THE BIG OCCASION COOK BOOK

Jan Arkless

Illustrated by Jill Waterman

RIGHT WAY

CONTENTS

For Amy Catriona and Jillian Lia,
because the Toddler's Tea is specially for you
xx

INTRODUCTION

'We really must celebrate – and have a good get-together.'
These are easy words to speak, until you start thinking seriously
of how you are going to cater for one or two dozen guests or
more, either in your own home, a marquee or a nearby hall.
Whether you prefer to cope on your own, or to organise plenty
of help from friends or relations, the ultimate responsibility
generally falls on one person – you! The suggested menus and
recipes in this book are designed to make your task easier: a
real doddle in fact! Many of the dishes can be prepared well in
advance (provided you have use of a freezer), and all the menus
proposed for each occasion can be interchanged, mixed and
matched, or adapted to suit your personal taste.

The menus are designed to cater for multiples of 12 people.
Simply add more or less as necessary to suit your numbers,
bearing in mind that small children and elderly people generally
eat less than hungry teenagers, and that men usually have larger
appetites than women; but in a family group this normally evens
out anyway. I chose units of 12 as that is often the maximum
you can squeeze around a normal dining table, and the number
you can cook for using normal family pans and dishes. If you
are catering for larger numbers, the buffet menus suggested
here (whether the guests eat at small tables or balance their
plates on their knees) are easy to manage.

Try to get organised early! Make lots of lists: for shopping
which needs doing well in advance (frozen foods, foil, packet
goods, paper napkins, etc.); and for last-minute shopping (fresh
fruit and vegetables). Decide which dishes you can prepare in
advance and store or freeze, and what you will have to do the
week before, the day before, and at the last minute on the day.
I stick the menu and check list up on the back of a cupboard
door in the kitchen and triumphantly tick off each item and dish
as it is prepared – it gives me a great feeling of achievement and
confidence that everything is going to be all right!

I hope all goes well on whatever occasion you're celebrating, and that everyone has a wonderful time – and don't forget to relax and enjoy your own party too!

1
PANIC PAGES

Helpful amounts to have handy when catering for larger numbers than usual. Of course, they're only approximate, depending on the occasion, and ages and appetites of the guests; after all, you know your family and friends much better than I do!

	Per Person	*For 12 People*
SOUP		
Depending on the occasion	5–10 fl oz/ 150–300ml	4–6 pints/ 2.5–3.5 litres
MEAT (BEFORE COOKING)		
Topside beef	6 oz/175g	4½–5 lb/2–2.25kg
Boned rolled lamb, pork or gammon	6 oz/175g	4½–5 lb/2–2.5kg joint
Lamb or pork on the bone	8 oz/225g	6–7 lb/2.5–3kg joint
Minced beef	4–6 oz/100–175g	3½–4½ lb/1.5–2kg
Turkey	12 oz/350g carved meat	11–12 lb/5kg turkey on the bone
Chicken	12 oz/350g	3 chickens (3–3½ lb/ 1.5kg each)
COLD COOKED MEATS		
Sliced ham/tongue	4 oz/100g	3 lb/1.5kg

	Per Person	*For 12 People*
Chicken quarters	1 each	12 pieces
Chicken drumsticks	2–3 each	24–36 pieces

FISH

Cold whole salmon	4–7 oz/100–200g sliced fish	5–6 lb/2.5–3kg whole salmon

PASTA

Dry, uncooked	3 oz/75g	2½ lb/1.25kg

RICE

Dry, uncooked	2–3 oz/50–75g	1½–2½ lb/700g–1kg
Cooked	4–6 oz/100–150g	3–5 lb/1.2–2kg

POTATOES

Before peeling	3–5 potatoes/ 8 oz/225g	6 lb/3kg

FROZEN VEGETABLES
PREPARED FRESH VEGETABLES

Peas, beans, sprouts, mixed vegetables	2–3 oz/50–75g	1½–2 lb/700–900g

FRESH VEGETABLES
BEFORE PREPARATION

Carrots, French and runner beans, broccoli, sprouts	4 oz/100g	3 lb/1.3kg
Broad beans, peas in pod	8 oz/225g	6 lb/2.5kg
Cauliflower		2 or 3 depending on size

Cabbage	2 or 3 depending on size
Broccoli	3–4 packs, depending on size of pack
Swede	2–3 large swedes

SAUSAGES
Chipolatas: 16 per 1 lb/450g pack
Thick sausages: 8 per 1 lb/450g pack

SALADS

All the following serve 12 people.

MIXED GREEN SALAD
Wash, slice if necessary, and toss in a large bowl: 2–3 lettuces (different kinds if possible, i.e. Iceberg, radicchio and round), 1 bunch watercress, 1 box cress, 1 bunch spring onions or 1 large onion, 1 bunch radishes, 1 red and 1 green pepper, 8 oz/225g tomatoes and 1 cucumber.

'GREEN' GREEN SALAD
Prepare as for a Mixed Green Salad above but only use green vegetables.

TOMATO SALAD
Slice 2½ lb/1kg tomatoes, cover with ¼ pint/150ml French dressing, and garnish with 1 bunch washed, chopped parsley.

RICE SALAD
Mix 1½ lb/700g cooked rice with one 330g can or 8 oz/225g cooked frozen peas and/or mixed vegetables. Stir in ½ pint/300ml French dressing.

COLESLAW
Finely slice 1½–2 lb/700g–1kg hard cabbage, shred 4 large carrots, finely chop 3–4 onions, slice 3–4 eating apples, and mix with ½ pint/300ml mayonnaise. Make a lovely nutty, crunchy

coleslaw by adding 4–8 oz/100–225g chopped salted nuts or halved walnuts and 1 head of celery, washed and chopped.

POTATO SALAD

Boil and slice 4½ lb/2kg potatoes, mix with ½ pint/300ml mayonnaise and 4 sliced hard-boiled eggs. Garnish with chopped fresh parsley.

MIXED BEAN SALAD

Drain and mix three 440g cans cooked beans (red kidney, cannellini, flageolet, barlotti – choose your favourites) with one 330g can drained sweetcorn, 2 finely chopped onions and 2–3 finely chopped celery sticks. Stir in ½ pint/300ml French dressing.

TABBOULEH

Soak 18 oz/500g bulgar wheat for approximately 1 hour and drain well (according to the instructions on the packet). Mix with a large bunch finely chopped spring onions (green and white), a large bunch chopped chives, a large bunch chopped parsley and a large bunch chopped mint. Mix in 8 fl oz/200ml good olive oil and the juice of 3 lemons. Season well with salt and pepper.

FRENCH DRESSING

Put ½ pint/300ml good olive oil or walnut oil into a large screwtop jar with 4–6 tblsp wine vinegar, 1 level tsp mustard powder, 1 level tsp sugar, salt and black pepper. Screw the lid on tight and shake well for several minutes to mix thoroughly. Store in the fridge until needed. Remove from the fridge an hour before serving so that it can reach room temperature. Toss the salad in the dressing just before serving or serve it in separate bowls or jugs.

MAYONNAISE

See the section on Eggs opposite first.

All ingredients must be at room temperature.

Put 2 egg yolks in a mixing bowl or mixer, and beat in ½ pint/300ml olive oil a few drops at a time. Season to taste with 1 tblsp lemon juice or wine vinegar, salt, black pepper, and a pinch of mustard if liked.

Garlic Mayonnaise
Add ½ tsp garlic powder with the seasonings.

Marie Rose Sauce
Add 1–2 tblsp tomato purée or tomato ketchup to the finished mayonnaise.

EGGS

In the light of worries over salmonella bacteria in eggs, make sure you buy eggs from a reputable supplier and heed government advice over the use, cooking and serving of eggs. Raw, or soft cooked, eggs are not recommended for babies, young children, pregnant women and the elderly.

I use size 2 eggs in my recipes unless specified otherwise.

BREAD
1 large sliced loaf = 26–30 slices.
1 French loaf   = 10–12 chunks; 2–3 loaves serve 12 people.
1 garlic loaf serves 4–6 people.

BUTTER

You will need one 250g pack softened butter or spreading margarine per loaf. Whipped butter goes further when making sandwiches.

CAKES AND DESSERTS

TRAY BAKES
These are great for children's parties and coffee mornings. The following makes 24 pieces.

Beat together 6 oz/175g sugar, 6 oz/175g margarine, 9 oz/250g self-raising flour, 2 tsp baking powder, 3 eggs, 4 tblsp milk for 2–3 minutes. Bake in a lined 13″ × 9″/31cm × 22cm Swiss roll tin for 30–35 minutes at 180°C/350°F/gas 4–5/fan 170°C. Cool in the tin, ice (see Butter Icing below) and cut into 24 pieces.

Chocolate
Replace the above quantity of flour with 8 oz/225g self-raising flour and 1 tblsp cocoa.

Coffee
Dissolve 2 tsp coffee powder in 2 tsp hot water, and add with the milk.

BUTTER ICING
Use 8 oz/225g icing sugar and 4 oz/100g margarine.

Chocolate
Beat in 2 tblsp drinking chocolate.

Coffee
Dissolve 2 tsp coffee powder in 2 tsp hot water. Cool and beat in.

GATEAU AND CHEESECAKE
One 8–9"/20–22cm cake cuts into 10–12 slices.

MERINGUES
A 4 egg quantity makes 24 meringue shells = 12 meringues.

PAVLOVA
A 3 egg quantity makes an 8–9"/20–22cm pavlova which serves 8–10 people. Fill with ½ pint/300ml double cream.

ECLAIRS
A 2 egg quantity makes 12 eclairs or 24 tray nibbles.

SCONES
A 1 lb/450g flour quantity makes 20–24 scones.

CAKE CASES
One pack of paper cases contains 60 cases.

PASTRY
A 1 lb/454g pack frozen puff pastry = 18 large/24 medium/30 small sausage rolls.

A 1 lb/500g pack frozen shortcrust pastry or
home-made shortcrust pastry made from
12 oz/350g flour
plus 1 lb/450g jar mincemeat

} makes 24 small mince pies

FLANS AND QUICHES
An 8″/20cm flan cuts into 8 average or 10 small servings.

A 9-10″/22–25cm flan cuts into 10 average or 12–14 small servings.

DRINKS

TEA
1 × 4 oz/100g pack = 10 tblsp/30 tsp

3 tblsp/9 tsp or 6 tea bags
and 3–3½ pints/2 litres
boiling water

} makes 12–16 cups of tea

COFFEE
Instant Coffee
1 × 200g jar instant coffee = 48 tblsp/144 tsp
= 144 cups of coffee

3 tblsp/12 tsp instant coffee
plus 3–3½ pints/2 litres
hot water

} makes 12–16 cups of coffee

Ground coffee
1 × 8 oz/225g pack ground coffee

= 36–40 dsp
= 36–40 medium cups of coffee or
= 72–80 tiny cups of coffee

9–12 dsp ground coffee plus
3–3½ pints/2 litres boiling
water

} makes 12–16 medium cups or 24–30 tiny cups of coffee

MILK
1 pint/0.5 litre = enough milk for 24–30 cups of tea or coffee

SUGAR
½ lb/225g/¼ packet sugar = 30 tsp
1kg packet sugar = 120 tsp

SQUASH AND FRUIT JUICE
1 litre bottle squash	= 30–40 glasses when diluted
1 litre diluted squash and water	= 4–6 glasses
1 pint diluted squash and water	= 3–4 glasses
1 litre pack fruit juice	= 6–9 glasses

SHERRY
Allow 1–2 glasses per person.

1 litre bottle = 12–16 glasses
1 75cl bottle = 8–10 glasses

Approximately 3 fl oz/85ml per glass. Allow 2–3 × 75cl bottles/
2 × 1 litre bottles for 12 people.

WINE
Allow 2–3 glasses/½ bottle per person (or more!)

1 litre bottle = 8–9 glasses
1 75cl bottle = 6–7 glasses

Approximately 4 fl oz/100ml per glass. Allow 5–6 × 75cl
bottles/3–4 × 1 litre bottles for 12 people.

CHAMPAGNE FOR TOASTS
Allow 1–2 glasses per person.

1 litre bottle = 8–10 glasses
1 75cl bottle = 6–8 glasses

Approximately 3–4 fl oz/85–100ml per glass. Allow 2–3 × 75cl
bottles/1–2 × 1 litre bottles for 12 people.

LIQUEURS
Allow 1–2 glasses per person.

1 litre bottle = 22–24 glasses
1 75cl bottle = 15–18 glasses

Approximately 1–1½ fl oz/30–40ml per glass. Allow 1–2 × 75cl bottles/1 × 1 litre bottle for 12 people.

P.S.

When preparing, cooking and storing food in advance, especially for large numbers which can be more difficult to cope with, please be particularly aware of the dangers of food poisoning, and of all the important and relevant aspects of good food hygiene – keeping food covered, refrigerating or chilling and freezing quickly, storing carefully and defrosting and serving sensibly. Try not to leave prepared food keeping warm on hotplates or standing on the table (particularly in a warm room) for long before the guests are ready to eat, and always keep everything covered until the last moment. Be especially careful when dealing with meat, fish, egg, rice and cream dishes. Also remember which dishes have been pre-frozen, and don't be tempted to refreeze any leftovers – anyway, there's usually someone who'll 'help you out' by taking some extras home for supper!!

There has been much discussion in the media recently about nuts and their fatal effect on people who are severely allergic to them. When catering for large numbers, particularly some people you may not know well, it would be wise to alert your guests to any dishes which contain nuts, either by labelling them on the buffet table, or verbally warning guests before they are served at the dinner table.

2

COMING OF AGE

Cold Finger Buffet to serve 24 people

A cold finger buffet is suitable for many occasions, from drinks with friends to a full-scale wedding reception. Although some preparation can be done in advance, time must be allowed on 'the day' for the assembly of much of the food, so I wouldn't recommend this menu for the mother of the bride unless she has plenty of reliable helpers.

Choose a selection of the suggested recipes to produce a varied and attractive menu according to personal taste and cost, bearing in mind the number and type of guests you are entertaining, and the fact that some people will appreciate the more sophisticated or unusual savouries, while others prefer traditional food. Remember also that young people, particularly the boys, are always hungry and have enormous appetites, so include some of the more filling dishes too.

I prefer a savoury menu for this type of party, but if you want some sweets or puds include the Chocolate Eclairs and Cream Meringues; or any of the desserts for the fork buffets (pages 45–

48 and 71–73) can be added to the menu.

Allow 10–15 pieces per person.

Fresh Salty Nuts *** Crisps *** Prawn Crackers, etc
Caviare or Lumpfish Roe with Lemon
Hummus and Taramasalata Dips
Mixed Canapés
Smoked Salmon and Asparagus Rolls
Stuffed Eggs
Celery and Cream Cheese Boats
Spicy Chicken Drumsticks
Cocktail Hedgehogs *** Cheese and Pineapple Sunshines
Savoury Eclairs
Open Bridge Rolls
Vol au Vents
Herby Sausage Rolls *** Cheese d'Artois
Savoury Filo Lucky Bags
Cheese Meringues *** Lemon Meringue Crisps
Chocolate Eclairs *** Cream Meringues
Coming of Age Cake

CHECK LISTS

THE MONTH BEFORE
Make and Freeze: Savoury and Sweet Eclairs (unfilled), Vol au Vent cases and Sauce, Herby Sausage Rolls, Cheese d'Artois, Savoury Filo Lucky Bags.

Buy and Freeze: Chicken legs and bread rolls.

Make/Buy and Store: Nuts for salting, crisps, prawn crackers, etc., canned goods, table linen and paper napkins. Make, buy or order the Coming of Age Cake well in advance, ready to put in the place of honour on the buffet table on the day. Buy or order soft and alcoholic drinks.

THE WEEK BEFORE
Buy as many of the ingredients as you can safely store in the fridge or cold larder to give you more time for food preparation on the day. (Cold meats, smoked salmon, salad stuffs and eggs can be stored for several days; check 'use by' dates when

buying.) Make Cheese and Sweet Meringue shells and store, unfilled, in airtight tins.

THE DAY BEFORE

Make topping spreads for Canapés and store in fridge. Hard-boil eggs for Stuffed Eggs, shell and prepare them for filling, and store in a plastic box in the fridge. Prepare cream cheese filling for Celery and Cream Cheese Boats; wash and trim celery. Make Lemon Meringue Crisps, cool and store in an airtight box. Cut cheese cubes for 'Hedgehogs', and store in the fridge. Make fillings for Savoury Eclairs, and Vol au Vents, and store in the fridge. Defrost and cook chicken drumsticks, and store in the fridge. Prepare spreads and toppings for Bridge Rolls, and store in the fridge. Wash parsley, watercress and lemons for garnishing, and store in plastic bags in the fridge.

THE EVENING BEFORE

Remove pastry dishes, bread and Vol au Vents Sauce from the freezer and leave to defrost ready for finishing in the morning. (The empty Eclairs will thaw quickly and can be defrosted in the morning.)

Set the buffet table if possible; assemble the glasses, plates, cutlery and napkins. Arrange any floral decorations and store in a cool place (perhaps the garage?), ready to put on the table at the last minute.

ON THE DAY

Prepare: Canapés, Salmon and Asparagus Rolls, Stuffed Eggs, Celery and Cream Cheese Boats, Open Bridge Rolls; dish, cover with cling film and keep cool until ready to serve. Prepare Cocktail Hedgehogs and Cheese and Pineapple Sunshines. Defrost Eclairs and fill Savoury Eclairs and Vol au Vent cases, and put aside to reheat before serving. Put Herby Sausage Rolls, Cheese d'Artois and Filo Lucky Bags ready to warm before serving. Cook Spicy Chicken Drumsticks if not prepared the day before. Dish Lemon Meringue Crisps. Fill Cheese and Sweet Meringues and dish; fill and ice Chocolate Eclairs, and dish. Prepare salty nuts and dish, with crisps, etc. Prepare Caviare or Lumpfish, and the dips.

AT THE LAST MINUTE
Heat and serve Savoury Eclairs, Vol au Vents, Sausage Rolls,
Cheese d'Artois and Filo Lucky Bags. Remove cling film from
all other foods and serve. Pour out the drinks, put on the music
and you're ready to party.

FRESH SALTY NUTS

*You'll need 2 lb/1kg for 24 people so cook a second batch of nuts
after the first, or make double the quantity if you have a very
large pan.*

These are best freshly made the same day you need them. Use
any mixture of fresh shelled nuts – perhaps make 1 lb/454g
peanuts and 1 lb/454g mixed nuts – because they are always very
popular and disappear fast. Add a little cayenne pepper or
curry powder to the salt if you want devilled nuts.

Making time: 5 minutes.

4–6 tblsp vegetable oil
2 oz/50g salted butter
1 lb/454g shelled fresh nuts – peanuts or mixed walnuts, Brazils,
    pecans, cashews, etc.
Salt for serving
Devilled nuts: 1 tsp cayenne pepper or curry powder

Heat the oil in a large, clean frying pan over a moderate heat.
Add the butter and, when foaming but not brown, add the nuts
and fry for 4–5 minutes, turning frequently with a slotted spoon
until the nuts are golden brown all over. Remove them from the
pan with a slotted spoon and drain well on kitchen paper.
Sprinkle with salt (and cayenne pepper or curry powder if used)
and serve warm or cold in one large bowl or several small
dishes.

CAVIARE OR LUMPFISH ROE WITH LEMON

You'll need 1½ lb/700g caviare or lumpfish to feed 24 people.

It depends on how special the occasion is! Lumpfish is less expensive than caviare. Place a glass bowl of chosen fish roe on a bed of ice (i.e. a second, larger, bowl filled with ice), and serve with a platter of small, salted or plain savoury biscuits and lemon slices. Let guests help themselves to the caviare by using a silver spoon.

HUMMUS AND TARAMASALATA DIPS

Buy 8–16 oz/225–454g good quality hummus and taramasalata from the supermarket or delicatessen and store in the fridge until needed. Pile the dips into bowls and serve with crisps and pitta bread (cut into small triangles). It's even nicer if you have time to warm the pittas in a toaster or oven just before serving.

MIXED CANAPÉS

Tiny savoury bites. Use a good variety of shapes, textures, colours and garnishes to provide a really attractive and appetising display. The toppings can be prepared the day before, but actually spread the canapés as late as possible before the guests are due, to serve them crisp and fresh.

Use crispbreads, savoury biscuits, crackers and toasts of different shapes and sizes as the base, or, if you have time and patience or a willing helper, toast crustless slices of white, brown and granary bread and cut them into squares, triangles and circles using a metal pastry cutter. Some of the fillings can be spread onto the dry toast or biscuit, but the wetter toppings are better if the base is buttered, to keep crisp.

SAVOURY BUTTERS
Beat 4 oz/100g butter with any of the following ingredients. Spread onto the canapé base and top or garnish with chosen ingredients.

Blue Cheese: Beat 2 oz/50g crumbled Stilton or Danish Blue cheese into softened butter. Top with half a walnut or chopped celery.

Chilli: Beat ½–1 tsp tabasco sauce (beware it's very hot) into the butter, with 1 tsp lemon juice. Top with a cucumber twist or radish slice.

Watercress: Makes a lovely green spread. Wash, dry and finely chop a generous handful of watercress and beat into the butter. Top with a small tomato chunk or a silver cocktail onion.

Garlic: Peel and press or finely chop 2 garlic cloves and beat into the butter (or use garlic powder or paste). Top with half a stuffed olive or a small strip of sweet pepper.

FISH TOPPINGS
Smoked Salmon: Spread with plain or savoury butter, top with a sliver of smoked salmon and a cucumber twist.

Caviare: Spread the bases with plain butter, then spoon a little roe on top of each biscuit.

Red Salmon: Drain an 8 oz/225g can of fish, remove the bones and flake slightly with a fork. Season with vinegar or lemon juice and black pepper, heap on the buttered bases, and garnish with watercress or cucumber.

Tuna: Drain a 7 oz/200g can of fish, mix with 2–3 tblsp mayonnaise or thick soured cream, season with black pepper, lemon juice or vinegar. Heap onto the buttered bases and garnish with a shake of paprika pepper.

CHEESY TOPPINGS
Cream Cheese and Cucumber: Mix 4 oz/100g cream cheese with a quarter of a finely chopped cucumber. Spread on plain biscuits and garnish with chopped chives or very finely snipped spring onions.

Cream Cheese and Onion: Mix 4 oz/100g cream cheese with a few washed, trimmed and finely chopped spring onions. Spread on plain bases, top with a shake of paprika pepper.

Cream Cheese and Chopped Nuts: Mix 4 oz/100g cream cheese with 2 oz/50g chopped mixed nuts. Spread on plain bases and top with half walnuts or a sliver of red or green pepper.

Cream Cheese and Egg: Hard-boil 2 or 3 eggs (see page 95), cool, peel and slice in an egg slicer. Spread the bases with cream cheese, top with a slice of egg and garnish with half a stuffed olive.

Grated Cheese and Onion: Mix 4 oz/100g grated Cheddar or other hard-type cheese with 1–2 tblsp mayonnaise or soft butter to make a stiff paste. Top the bases generously and garnish with a strip of sliced onion.

Plain Cheese: Top the buttered bases with a slice of cheese of your choice – blue cheese always looks attractive – and garnish with tomato or pepper, or leave plain.

OTHER TOPPINGS
Mushroom: Spread the biscuits with plenty of garlic or watercress butter, and top with a few slices of washed, thinly sliced button mushrooms.

Egg (1): Hard-boil 2 or 3 eggs (see page 95), cool, peel and mash with 2 tblsp mayonnaise and/or 1–2 tsp tomato purée or ketchup. Heap on top of buttered biscuits or toasts, and garnish with a strip of tomato.

Egg (2): Or soft scramble 2 or 3 eggs in a pan with a little butter, and season well with salt and pepper. When cold, heap onto buttered bases and garnish with a little chopped celery.

SMOKED SALMON AND ASPARAGUS ROLLS
Makes 30–36.

These are luxurious but expensive made with smoked salmon. For a cheaper alternative, make Plain Asparagus Rolls, using granary bread and butter instead of salmon, or make a mixture. They should be prepared on the day as they are not suitable for freezing.

Preparation time: 15 minutes.

2 × 15 oz/430g cans large asparagus spears
Either 1 lb/450g thinly sliced smoked salmon
   Or 1 small granary or brown loaf with 4 oz/100g butter
1 lemon to garnish

Drain the asparagus, and cut each spear in half. Cut the salmon slices into 3"/7.5cm squares, or cut thin slices of bread, remove the crusts, butter each slice and cut into squares as for the salmon. Lay a piece of asparagus on each slice of salmon or bread and roll up securely. Arrange on a serving platter, garnish with lemon slices and cover with cling film. Keep cool until ready to serve.

Using fresh asparagus is even better, but unless you live near asparagus fields or grow your own, it makes a very expensive dish. Steam trimmed, fresh asparagus for 5–10 minutes until tender, and cool before making into rolls.

STUFFED EGGS   *Makes 24.*

Quick and easy. Prepare the eggs and the fillings the day
before, store in the fridge and assemble on the day.

Preparation and cooking time: 30 minutes.

12 eggs
¼ pint/150ml mayonnaise
2 tsp tomato purée or ketchup (optional)
2 tsp curry paste and dash tabasco sauce (optional)
Salt, black pepper
Few stuffed olives and/or 2 tomatoes to garnish
Paprika pepper

Hard-boil the eggs (see page 95), cool and shell carefully. Halve
the eggs lengthwise and scoop out the yolks. Mash the yolks
with a fork and mix to a thick paste with the mayonnaise.
Flavour with the tomato purée or curry paste if liked (or make
some of each), and season with salt and pepper. Cover and
store the egg whites and fillings in the fridge.

To serve: Pile the egg yolk mixture into each egg white and fork
neatly, or pipe the filling in a piping bag using a ½"/1.25cm star
tube. Decorate with half olives or pieces of tomato, and a shake
of paprika. Arrange on a serving dish, cover loosely with cling
film and keep cool until ready to serve.

CELERY AND CREAM CHEESE BOATS
Makes 36.

The celery can be washed and trimmed the day before, and the filling prepared and stored in the fridge.

Preparation time: 15 minutes.

1 head white celery
8 oz/225g cream cheese or drained cottage cheese
4 oz/100g chopped nuts (optional – see page 15)
4 oz/100g small frozen prawns (optional)
1 small (2 oz/50g) can anchovies (optional)

Wash and trim the celery. Put the cream or drained cottage cheese into a basin and stir in the nuts if used. Store in the fridge until needed.

To serve: Defrost and drain prawns if using. Mix them into the chosen cheese. Cut the prepared celery into 2″/5cm lengths and spoon some cheese mixture into each 'boat'. Garnish with a piece of drained anchovy if liked. Arrange on a serving dish, cover loosely with cling film and keep in the fridge until needed.

SPICY CHICKEN DRUMSTICKS
Allow 1 or 2 per person.

Buy large packs of chilled or frozen chicken drumsticks which can be quickly prepared on the day and served warm or cold.

Prepare and serve as on page 88, but sprinkle the drumsticks with 1–2 packets spicy chicken seasoning mixed with the dried herbs before cooking. Either cook the chicken the day before (or earlier on the day), drain on kitchen paper, cool, dish and refrigerate until needed and serve cold; or cook just before serving and serve warm – ON NO ACCOUNT 'RE-WARM' COOKED CHICKEN. Serve garnished with parsley, and plenty of paper napkins.

COCKTAIL HEDGEHOGS

Makes 64 'bites'.

I prefer to use chipolata sausages, cut in half and eaten cold, but you may prefer to use canned Frankfurter sausages.

Preparation and cooking time: 30 minutes.

2–3 large, oval potatoes – well washed
2 lb/2 × 454g pack chipolata sausages
  Or 3–4 (8–10 sausage) cans Frankfurter sausages
1 200g jar small pickled or silver onions
Cocktail sticks

Prepare the Cocktail Hedgehogs as for Sausage Hedgehogs (see page 97) and add the drained onions speared onto sticks among the sausages. If using Frankfurters, cook as instructed on the can, drain and serve as chipolatas.

CHEESE AND PINEAPPLE SUNSHINES
Makes about 48 'bites'.

Prepare the cheese chunks in advance and store in the fridge. Use any mixture of hard Cheddar-type cheeses, preferably in two contrasting colours. The pineapple can be on separate sticks or speared with the cheese.

Preparation time: 15 minutes.

8 oz/225g pale Cheddar cheese
8 oz/225g Red Leicester or contrasting colour cheese
1 × 15 oz/454g can pineapple slices
Cocktail sticks
1 large grapefruit

Prepare the 'Sunshines' as per page 98. Serve on small plates without the cotton wool clouds!

ECLAIRS – SAVOURY AND SWEET

Makes 24 tiny nibbles; if you prefer, make double so that everyone has a couple.

Fill with a savoury mixture as for Vol au Vents, or with whipped cream and a chocolate or coffee icing on top. Fill and ice eclairs on the day as they may go soft if stored too long once filled.

Preparation and cooking time: 40–45 minutes.

2 oz/50g margarine
¼ pint/150ml water
2½ oz/62g plain flour
2 large eggs – well beaten
Large piping bag and plain ½"/1.25cm pipe

Heat the oven at 200°C/400°F/gas 6–7/fan 190°C and grease two baking sheets. Put the margarine and water into a medium-sized saucepan and bring to the boil (the mixture should be quite bubbly). Remove from the heat, add all the flour at once, and beat well with a wooden spoon; the mixture should form a thick paste. Gradually beat in all the beaten egg to produce a thick, shiny mixture. Spoon the mixture into the prepared piping bag, and pipe 24 eclairs, 1–1½"/2–3cm long, onto the baking sheets, leaving room for them to rise. Bake in the hot oven for 15–20 minutes until puffed up and golden (the inside should be almost hollow).

Cool on a wire tray after making a tiny hole in the side of each eclair with a skewer to let the steam out. When cold, fill with the chosen filling, or store unfilled in an airtight box for 3–4 days, or freeze unfilled until needed.

To serve: Defrost completely if frozen.

SAVOURY ECLAIRS
Fill carefully with any of the fillings used for Vol au Vents (see pages 29–30). Heat the filled eclairs in a hot oven, as above, for 5–10 minutes until warmed through. Garnish the tops with a

shake of paprika or a sprinkle of snipped parsley, and arrange on a serving dish.

SWEET ECLAIRS
Whip ½ pint/300ml double cream until very stiff, and fill each tiny eclair generously. Make coffee or chocolate water icing (put 8 oz/225g sieved icing sugar into a basin, dissolve 2 tsp cocoa or 1 heaped tsp instant coffee in a very little hot water and mix into the icing sugar, adding a little more hot water if needed to make a thick icing). Spread a little on each filled eclair and leave to set. Arrange on a serving platter and keep cool until needed.

OPEN BRIDGE ROLLS   *36 halves.*

This will provide a 'good filling' snack, particularly useful if you have a lot of large young men to feed, when you may decide to make double quantity! Prepare rolls on the day, although the toppings can be prepared and stored in the fridge the day before. The Club Sandwiches (see page 52), cut small, would also be suitable for this party.

18 finger-shaped bread rolls
1 × 250g pack butter (softened) or low fat spread

Toppings
Use any of the canapé spreads or toppings (see pages 20–22) or Club Sandwich fillings (see page 53). I would also provide some quite plain rolls topped with slices of cooked meats and decorated with a minimum of salad, as there's always someone who doesn't like 'all this fancy food'!

To serve: Arrange the rolls or sandwiches on large serving platters, garnish and cover with cling film. Keep in a cool place until needed.

VOL AU VENTS

Makes 36; if you prefer, make double so that everyone has a couple.

The pastry cases and the sauce can be made in advance and frozen separately, ready to be assembled and heated on the day. Mix and match from the variety of fillings suggested below. The fillings may be made the day before and stored in the fridge until needed.

PASTRY CASES

Preparation and cooking time: 20–25 minutes.

36 smallest size frozen vol au vent cases

Cook according to the instructions on the pack. Cool on a wire tray. Fill if using immediately or open freeze the empty cases, then pack them carefully into plastic boxes and return to the freezer.

FILLINGS

Thick White Sauce
Preparation and cooking time: 10 minutes.

1 heaped tblsp cornflour
½ pint/300ml milk
1 oz/25g butter or margarine
Salt, black pepper

Mix the cornflour in a basin with a little of the milk, to make a smooth paste. Heat the rest of the milk, pour onto the cornflour paste, stirring all the time. Return the mixture to the pan and reheat, stirring until the mixture thickens. Beat in the butter or margarine, and season well with salt and pepper. The sauce may be frozen plain and the fillings stirred in after defrosting, or stir the fillings into the sauce and use at once.

Cheese: Add 8 oz/225g grated mature Cheddar cheese and a good pinch of mustard, beat well until smooth.

Chicken: Stir in 8 oz/225g cooked, diced chicken.

Ham: Stir in 8 oz/225g cooked diced ham.

Mushrooms: Wash and slice 8 oz/225g mushrooms, sauté in a little butter for 3–4 minutes, drain and add to the sauce.

Prawn: Defrost 8 oz/225g small prawns, drain well and stir into the sauce. Use the same day; do not refreeze the prawns.

Sweetcorn: Add two 330g cans sweetcorn to the sauce and season with a pinch of cayenne pepper if liked, or add a little drained sweetcorn to any of the other fillings.

Instant Filling: Instead of making white sauce, use two 418g cans chicken in cream sauce, adding any of the other fillings as preferred.

To serve: Stir the fillings into the fresh or defrosted sauce, warming the defrosted sauce if necessary to make it easier to beat smooth again. Fill the fresh or defrosted pastry cases generously with the sauce and top with their pastry lids. Stand the filled cases on baking trays and reheat thoroughly in a hot oven (200°C/400°F/gas 6–7/fan 190°C) for 10 minutes just before serving. Arrange on a serving plate and garnish with fresh snipped parsley, cress or watercress.

HERBY SAUSAGE ROLLS

Makes 30–36 tiny rolls; if you prefer, make double so that you have plenty as these are very popular!

Preparation and cooking time: 1 hour.

1 lb/454g pack puff pastry – defrosted
1 lb/454g sausage meat or de-skinned sausages
1 small onion – peeled and very finely chopped or grated
2 tsp mixed herbs
Handful fresh, finely snipped parsley
Milk for brushing

Heat the oven at 200°C/400°F/gas 6–7/fan 190°C. Cut the pastry in half and roll each piece into an oblong 12″/30cm by 16″/40cm. Cut each piece in half longways to give four strips. Put the sausage meat into a basin, and mash in the onion, herbs and a little parsley. Divide into four and, using a little flour on your hands, roll into four long sausages to fit the lengths of pastry. Place a sausage on one side of each pastry strip, brush the edges with milk and roll the pastry over to enclose the sausage, ending up with the 'seam' underneath. Press firmly to seal and cut each long sausage into 7–9 tiny rolls. Put on a baking tray, seams underneath, and shape neatly. Brush the tops with milk, cut 2 or 3 slits in the top of each, and bake in the hot oven for 10 minutes until the pastry starts to colour. Then reduce the heat to 180°C/350°F/gas 4–5/fan 170°C and cook for a further 10–15 minutes until the pastry is golden and the sausage is cooked. Cool on a wire tray, open freeze, then store in the freezer in a plastic box.

To serve: Defrost thoroughly, then heat through in the hot oven (200°C/400°F/gas 6–7/fan 190°C) for 5–10 minutes (check that the pastry does not get too brown). Garnish with parsley and serve warm.

P.S. If you're short of time, buy frozen sausage rolls. Defrost, cut each roll into 1½″/4cm lengths, and bake, freeze and serve as home-made rolls above.

CHEESE D'ARTOIS

Makes 24 fingers; if you prefer, make double as these 'cheese straws' are 'moreish'!

A delicious meatless alternative to the ever-popular sausage roll.

Preparation and cooking time: 45–50 minutes.

8 oz/225g pack puff pastry – defrosted
4 oz/100g margarine
8 oz/225g grated mature Cheddar cheese
Good pinch cayenne pepper, mustard and salt
1 egg – beaten
Milk for brushing

Heat the oven at 200°C/400°F/gas 6–7/fan 190°C. Cut the pastry in half and roll each piece into an oblong 8"/20cm by 12"/30cm, about ⅛"/3mm thick. Cut each strip in half longways. Melt the margarine in a pan over a low heat. Remove from the heat and stir in the cheese and seasonings, and mix to a thick paste with the beaten egg. Put two pastry strips onto a baking sheet. Spread equally with the cheese filling, cover with the remaining pastry strips and pinch the edges together. Mark diagonal lattice lines carefully on top with a sharp knife, and cut three-quarters of the way through into the pieces. Brush with milk or milk and egg (use up any unused egg from the filling), and bake for 10–15 minutes until golden brown. Cool on a wire tray, cut into fingers and freeze.

To serve: Defrost, put the cheese fingers onto a baking tray and warm in the hot oven (200°C/400°F/gas 6–7/fan 190°C) for 5–10 minutes. Pile onto a serving dish, garnish with paprika and serve warm.

SAVOURY FILO LUCKY BAGS
Makes 12 of each filling.

An unusual, tasty savoury.

Preparation and cooking time: 30–40 minutes.

24 sheets filo pastry – chilled fresh or defrosted
Approximately 8 oz/225g butter – melted but not hot

Fillings
(1) 8 oz/225g goat's cheese roll, cut into 12 pieces
     12 tsp mango chutney
(2) 12 small Camembert triangles
     12 tsp Cranberry sauce

Use the filo pastry according to the instructions on the packet, keeping it covered when not being used. Unroll one sheet filo and brush with the melted butter, fold in half and brush again. Put a slice of the chosen cheese in the middle, top with the sauce, and gently pull the pastry together to make a bag, pinching the corners together to stop the filling from escaping and squeezing carefully into a lucky bag shape. Brush again with melted butter and put onto a freezer tray or a greased baking sheet. Make 24 bags, and cook at once or open freeze uncooked (it's best if you can leave them on the tray as they're quite fragile), defrosting on the day to cook and serve.

To cook and serve: Defrost. Heat the oven at 210°C/410°F/gas 6–7/fan 200°C. Bake the lucky bags on greased trays for 8–10 minutes until just crisp and golden. They're delicious served hot, but they can be cooked in the morning and just warmed through with the sausage rolls prior to serving. Any spare Vol au Vent filling can be used up in the lucky bags.

MERINGUES – SAVOURY OR SWEET

Each egg white makes 8–10 shells.

Cheesy meringues can be added to the savoury buffet table; the sweet ones can be served as a dessert. The meringues can be made well in advance and filled on the day, but don't fill them too early or they may go soft.

Preparation and cooking time: 1½–2 hours.

SAVOURY
For each egg white use 1½ oz/40g grated strong Cheddar cheese with a tsp grated Parmesan mixed in for a strong 'bite'.
Pinch salt, pinch mustard powder
Cream cheese to sandwich together
Paprika to garnish

SWEET
For each egg white allow 2 oz/50g castor sugar
Whipped cream – ¼ pint/150ml double cream will sandwich 16–20 tiny meringues
2 oz/50g chopped nuts or flaked almonds to garnish (see page 15)
Or 2–3 tsp drinking chocolate powder

Heat the oven at 100°C/200°F/gas ¼–½/fan 90°C. Line one or two baking trays with oiled greaseproof paper or baking parchment.

SAVOURY
Mix the grated cheese, salt and mustard in a basin. Whisk the egg whites using a whisk, mixer or processor until very stiff and dry. Use a metal spoon and fold the cheese mixture into the egg. Drop small spoonfuls of meringue onto the prepared sheets, making tiny shell shapes, leaving space between. Bake for 1–1½ hours until pale golden, crisp and dry. Remove from the paper, cool on a wire tray and store in an airtight tin; the shells will keep crisp for several weeks if stored in a dry place.

To serve: Sandwich together on the day with cream cheese, garnish with paprika and arrange on a serving dish. Store in a dry place (not the fridge) until needed.

SWEET
Whisk the egg whites with a whisk, mixer or processor until stiff and forming soft peaks. Continue whisking, adding sugar 1 tsp at a time until it is all whisked in. Drop in small shell shapes onto prepared baking sheets, leaving space between and bake and store as for Savoury Meringues.

To serve: Sandwich together just before serving, with stiffly whipped cream and put into pretty paper cases. Decorate with a few chopped or flaked nuts or a shake of drinking chocolate powder. Arrange on a serving dish and store in a cool, dry place.

LEMON MERINGUE CRISPS

Makes 18; if you prefer, make double so that you have plenty.

A light, unusual snack I first tasted in Florida.

Preparation and cooking time: 30 minutes.

3 tblsp ground almonds (see page 15)
3 tblsp Parmesan cheese
2 tsp grated lemon rind
2 egg whites
Parsley or lemon slices to garnish

Heat the oven at 150°C/300°F/gas 2–3/fan 140°C. Line one or two baking trays with oiled greaseproof paper or baking parchment.

Mix the ground almonds, Parmesan cheese and lemon rind. Beat the egg whites with a whisk or mixer until stiff but not dry. Then carefully fold the cheese mixture into the whipped whites using a metal spoon. Drop the meringue mixture in small spoonfuls onto the prepared trays and bake for 15–20 minutes until pale but crisp. Turn off the heat, open the oven door and leave the crisps in the oven until quite cold. Remove from the baking paper and store in an airtight tin until needed; do not store in the fridge or they will go soft.

To serve: Arrange on a serving dish, and garnish with parsley or lemon slices.

3

SMALL INFORMAL
WEDDING RECEPTION

Cold Fork Buffet to serve 48 people

A simple but delicious menu, easily prepared in advance, leaving the minimum to do on the day (provided that you have plenty of room in your freezer of course!). If I ever get to be the mother of the bride, doing the catering myself, this is the menu I'd choose for a reception at home, in a marquee, or in the village hall, as I'd want time to enjoy 'The Day' myself. I'd hope to arrange plenty of helpers to do the last-minute assembling of the dishes and to set out the buffet while the wedding party was at the ceremony.

Choose a selection of dishes according to cost and personal taste; the number of average-sized servings is given with each recipe. Try and provide as much seating as possible, whether a formal plan or just tables and chairs, as it's more comfortable to eat fork food sitting at a table than balancing plate, fork and glass – especially when wearing wedding finery and your biggest hat!

Cold Turkey *** Cold Roast Beef *** Cold Roast Gammon
Fresh Salmon Mayonnaise
Egg and Bacon Pie *** Stilton, Walnut and Vegetable Flan
'Green' Green Salad (page 9) *** Mixed Bean Salad (page 10)
Rice Salad (page 9) *** Tabbouleh (page 10)
Potato Salad (page 10) *** Nutty Coleslaw (page 9)
French Bread *** Mixed Bread Rolls
Butter *** Low Fat Spread
Mayonnaise *** French Dressing
Chocolate Lemon Cheesecake *** Mary's Grape Pavlova
Posh Fruit Salad
Thick Cream *** Greek Yoghurt
Cheese Boards
Wedding Cake

CHECK LISTS

AT LEAST 2 MONTHS BEFORE
The Wedding Cake should be made or ordered well in advance, as rich fruit cakes should be stored for at least 2 months to allow the wonderful flavour to develop. If you are decorating the cake yourself, try and have it finished just the week before, so that it will remain fresh and beautiful for the day, but will not leave you worrying over it at the last minute. Also, buy or hire the cake stand and special knife, to make it look really attractive.

THE MONTH BEFORE
You will probably need to 'borrow' space in friends' and neighbours' fridges, freezers and larders this month.
   Make/Cook and Freeze: Turkey, Beef, Gammon, Egg and Bacon Pie, Chocolate Lemon Cheesecake.
   Buy and Store/Order: Flowers and table decorations. Arrange to hire or borrow glasses, china, cutlery, serving dishes and table linen. Order Salmon Mayonnaise. Buy wines and soft drinks.

THE WEEK BEFORE
Buy/Make and Store: Freeze bread and rolls. Make mayonnaise and French dressing and store in the fridge. Make Pavlova

bases and store in airtight containers. Buy plenty of butter and low fat spread. Buy cheeses for cheese boards, fruit for fruit salad, salad ingredients, cream and Greek yoghurt.

THE DAY BEFORE
Cook/Prepare: Cook the meat and poultry if not pre-frozen. Prepare salad vegetables and store in the fridge. Prepare fruit for Pavlovas. Buy bread and rolls if not pre-frozen. Collect Salmon Mayonnaise and store in the fridge.

THE EVENING BEFORE
Defrost: Cooked meats, poultry, Egg and Bacon Pie, Stilton and Walnut Flan.

Make table decorations and floral arrangements and store in a cool place. Set tables for the buffet and for sitting at. If possible, have a small, separate table for the cake. Arrange glasses and drinks, put wines to chill, and put out serving dishes and plates. Arrange to have two identical serving places to avoid huge queues in one place.

ON THE DAY
Try and get up early and have most of the panic over before the bride appears!

Defrost: Bread, rolls and Chocolate Lemon Cheesecake.

Assemble and Dish: Cold meats, salmon, pies, flans, salads, mayonnaise, salad dressing, fruit salad. Decorate or garnish and cover with cling film. Whip cream and finish Pavlovas and store in a cool place. Whip extra cream and dish; also dish yoghurt. Prepare and garnish cheese boards. Arrange the food on the buffet table, removing the cling film at the last minute, leaving the desserts in a cool place until required. Set up the Wedding Cake. Try and leave the final arrangements in the capable hands of your helpers and go off and enjoy getting yourself, and the bride, ready for the Church or Registry Office.

COLD MEATS

The amount of meat you buy will depend on how many other savouries you are serving with the salads, remembering that most people will want to try a little of everything. Cook meat and poultry in advance, allow it to cool and carve when cold to get thin, neat slices.

TURKEY

If serving just turkey as the main meat, buy two 18–20 lb (8.25–9kg) turkeys to provide 48 generous helpings. If serving a variety of meats and savouries, one large turkey should be sufficient.

Defrost thoroughly, then roast according to the instructions on the wrapper. Cool quickly and carve, keeping the white and brown meat separate for easier dishing later. Wrap in cling film and refrigerate or freeze.

BEEF

This is a rather expensive choice, so consult your butcher as to the best buy. (Brian and Keith in our village shop are always very helpful.) I would buy whole rolled topsides, which weigh 6½–7 lb (3kg) approximately. If serving only beef, you would need three joints of this size for 48 generous helpings. If serving with other meats, one or two should be enough.

Roast in a hot oven (200°C/400°F/gas 6–7/fan 190°C), allowing 15–20 minutes per pound (450g). Under- rather than over-cook the joint as it will continue to cook in its own heat as it cools. Cool quickly, carve thinly and put the slices back into a joint shape, so that the juices are retained within the meat. Wrap in cling film and refrigerate or freeze.

GAMMON

Buy joints of middle cut green (unsmoked) gammon, allowing the same weights as for beef (see above). Soak for an hour in cold water, then wrap the joint loosely into a foil parcel and put in a baking tin. Roast in a moderate oven (180°C/350°F/gas 4–5/fan 170°C), allowing 20 minutes per pound (450g). Take out of the oven, remove the skin and spread thickly with a paste of brown sugar and mustard (6 tblsp soft brown sugar, 2–3 tsp mustard), score fat into diamonds and bake, uncovered, for a further 20 minutes to brown the outside nicely. Cool, carve and store as for beef.

To serve Cold Meats: Defrost if pre-frozen, arrange slices of meat on large serving platters, cover with cling film and keep cool until ready to serve.

FRESH SALMON MAYONNAISE

This needs to be very freshly cooked and garnished on the day. As you will be very busy that morning, I would buy this ready-prepared to serve from the delicatessen counter of one of the large, reliable supermarkets now offering this service. The fish are cooked and beautifully garnished with mayonnaise, cucumber and possibly prawns, ready to put onto the buffet table.

If only serving salmon and no meat, order four 6 lb/3kg fish. If serving with a variety of meats and savouries, then two fish should be enough (this is one dish that most people will wish to taste).

EGG AND BACON PIE   *Serves 10–12 so make 2 or 3.*

Prepare and freeze in advance, serve hot or cold.

Preparation and cooking time: 1–1¼ hours.

8 oz/225g flour quantity shortcrust pastry
   or 1 × 1 lb/500g pack frozen shortcrust pastry – defrosted
8 rashers streaky bacon – de-rinded and trimmed
4 eggs
4 tomatoes – sliced
4 oz/100g mushrooms – washed and sliced
Handful fresh parsley – washed and snipped
Salt, black pepper, milk for brushing

Heat the oven at 200°C/400°F/gas 6–7/fan 190°C. Roll out two-thirds of the pastry and line the base and sides of a 9–10″/22–25cm flan tin. Prick the pastry all over and spread the bacon pieces in a single layer over the base. Crack the eggs and either pour them as they are (whole) over the bacon, or beat them well and then pour over the bacon. Cover with sliced tomatoes and mushrooms, sprinkle on parsley and season well.

Roll out the rest of the pastry to form the lid, and cover the pie, trimming the edges, pinching well together and fluting prettily. Roll out any pastry scraps and cut into leaves to decorate the top. Brush with milk and bake in the hot oven for 15 minutes. Then reduce the heat to 180°C/350°F/gas 4–5/fan 170°C for a further 30 minutes until the pastry is golden and the filling is cooked. Cool in the tin and freeze, as it can be removed from the tin more easily when frozen.

To serve: Defrost very thoroughly. Serve cold or heat in the moderate oven as before (180°C/350°F/gas 4–5/fan 170°C) for 15 minutes and then serve.

STILTON, WALNUT AND VEGETABLE FLAN
Serves 10–12 so make 2 or 3.

A substantial savoury flan suitable as a main course for vegetarians or as a tasty addition to the meat course. Make and freeze in advance, to cook through on the day.

Preparation and cooking time: 45 minutes.

6 oz/175g flour quantity shortcrust pastry or
 1 × 13 oz/350g pack frozen shortcrust pastry – defrosted
1 lb/450g leeks – trimmed, washed and sliced
4 oz/100g frozen mixed vegetables ⎫ or 8 oz/225g
1 × 300g can sweetcorn   ⎬   frozen vegetables
4 oz/100g Stilton cheese   ⎭
¾ pint/450ml double cream or canned sterilised cream
4 oz/100g roughly chopped or broken walnuts (see page 15)
4 oz/100g mature Cheddar cheese

Roll out the pastry and use it to line a deep 10″/25cm flan dish, prick and bake blind (lining the pastry with foil) for 10–15 minutes in a hot oven (190°C/375°F/gas 5–6/fan 180°C) until crisp and golden.

Cook the leeks in a very little boiling water for 3–5 minutes until cooked but still crisp. Cook the frozen vegetables in boiling water for 2–3 minutes. Drain all the vegetables very well.

Crumble the Stilton and put in a large saucepan with the cream, heat gently until the cheese melts and the cream simmers. Remove from the heat, stir in the cooked vegetables, drained sweetcorn and chopped nuts. Pour into the flan case, sprinkle with grated Cheddar cheese. Open freeze, to defrost and cook on the day.

To serve: Defrost the flan, bake in a hot oven as above (190°C/ 350°F/gas 5–6/fan 180°C) for 15 minutes to melt the cheese topping. Serve warm, garnished with watercress.

SALADS

See page 9. Make double amounts of each salad, as most people like to try a little of everything. Prepare the following and store in the fridge, to assemble and serve on the day: wash and prepare the salad vegetables; boil, cool and slice the potatoes; boil and peel the eggs; mix the French dressing (see below); make the mayonnaise (see below).

MAYONNAISE

See page 10. Allow 1½–2 pints/900–1200ml. Pile into bowls and place on the buffet table.

FRENCH DRESSING

See page 10. Allow 2 pints/1200ml. To ensure crisp green salad, the lettuces must be tossed at the last minute, but I like to serve the dressing separately, in small jugs or bowls with ladles or spoons, as some people prefer their salad plain.

BREAD

Buy French bread and rolls in advance and store in the freezer if you have room. Buy sealed packs the day before or order locally and arrange for someone to collect the fresh bread on the day (you certainly won't have time to dash round the supermarket before the wedding). Allow 8 long French loaves, cut into thick slices on the day and piled in baskets or bowls on the buffet table, or serve a mixture of bread and brown, white and granary rolls.

BUTTER

Allow 6 (250g size) packets of butter with 2 (250g size) packets of low fat spread; this should be ample to serve with the cheese as well.

CHOCOLATE LEMON CHEESECAKE
Serves 8–10, so make several!

Looks wonderful, topped with a few fresh strawberries or raspberries or simply a twist of lemon. Freezes well and just needs the fruit garnish on the day.

Preparation and cooking time: 20 minutes, plus setting time.

4 oz/100g butter
8 oz/225g plain chocolate digestive biscuits – finely crushed

Topping
8 oz/225g cream cheese
3–4 tblsp lemon juice, or to taste
½ pint/300ml double cream – whipped
1 tblsp castor sugar, or to taste

Heat the oven at 160°C/325°F/gas 3–4/fan 150°C. Melt the butter over a low heat, stir in the biscuit crumbs and press into a greased 9–10″/22–25cm deep flan ring or spring clip tin. Bake for 8–10 minutes, remove from the oven and cool completely in the tin.

Beat the cream cheese with 2 tblsp lemon juice and 1 tblsp whipped cream until soft and creamy. Fold in the remaining whipped cream and add lemon juice and sugar to taste. Spoon over the cold flan base, leave in a cold place to set, or freeze in the tin (it can be removed from the flan tin more easily when frozen).

To serve: Defrost completely, arrange on a serving dish and decorate with a twist of lemon or a few fresh strawberries or raspberries if available (if you're serving fruit Pavlovas as well I'd use the lemon garnish for a contrast). Keep cool until ready to serve.

MARY'S GRAPE PAVLOVA
Serves 8–10, so make several!

A Plymouth neighbour's party special. Pavlovas are always popular and look very pretty on the buffet table. Make all grape toppings or use several different fruits; any combination of fruit folded into the whipped cream is delicious. The meringue bases can be made several days in advance and the different toppings quickly added on the day.

Preparation and cooking time: 1 hour 15–30 minutes.

MERINGUE

Silicone baking paper
3 large egg whites
6 oz/175g castor sugar
1 tsp cornflour
1 tsp malt vinegar
½ tsp vanilla essence

Heat the oven at 150°C/300°F/gas 2–3/fan 140°C. Put silicone paper onto a greased baking tray and mark out an 8–9"/20–22cm circle (use a plate to draw round).

Whip the egg whites until stiff, then whisk in the sugar 1 tsp at a time. Mix the cornflour with the vinegar and vanilla, and beat in with the last of the sugar. Spoon the thick, creamy mixture onto the marked circle and spread gently and lightly to make a solid base with slightly raised sides.

Bake in the low oven for about 1 hour until a very pale creamy colour. (If making several Pavlovas, fill all the oven shelves and cook 2 or 3 bases together.) Turn the oven off and leave the Pavlova in the oven until cold. Carefully peel the cold Pavlova from the baking paper and store in an airtight container until needed. Large sheets of foil can be used as an airtight 'tent' if necessary.

To serve: On the day, put the meringue on a serving dish and top with chosen fruit and cream (see below). Decorate with fresh mint leaves.

TOPPINGS
For each Pavlova use ½ pint/300ml double cream, whipped until stiff but not solid, mixed with chosen fruit.

Grape

8 oz/225g grapes, halved and de-seeded if necessary
A mean ½ glass pale, sweet sherry

Put the halved grapes into a basin with the sherry, cover and leave to soak for an hour, or overnight. Strain the grapes, stir the sherry syrup into the whipped cream, pile into the Pavlova and top with the drained grapes, mixing them in slightly but not entirely covering them all.

Strawberry or Raspberry

8 oz/225g fresh strawberries or fresh/frozen raspberries

Reserving a few berries for decoration, hull and halve the strawberries or pick over the raspberries, and fold them carefully into the whipped cream, adding 1–2 tblsp castor sugar to taste, if liked. Pile onto the meringue and decorate with the reserved berries.

Kiwi

4 kiwi fruits, peeled

Chop 3 of the kiwi fruits into dice and fold into the thick cream. Pile them onto the meringue base. Slice the remaining fruit and arrange the slices on top of the cream.

POSH FRUIT SALAD
Makes 1 huge bowlful, so make 2 lots!

For a special buffet this has got to look spectacular, not a mish-mash of bits of fruit languishing in syrup! If any other special fresh fruits are available, add them to the suggested list below. People will eat it on its own, or take a little with the other desserts, so it's always very popular. To be at its best it needs assembling on the day, but the fruit can be prepared and stored the day before and kept in the fridge.

Preparation time: 30 minutes. Standing time: 1–2 hours.

2 or 3 different melons – Honeydew, Ogen, Charentais, Galia
½ water melon
8 oz/225g green grapes – seedless or de-seeded
8 oz/225g black grapes – de-seeded
3–4 kiwi fruits
2–3 nectarines – wash but do not peel
2–3 peaches – wash but do not peel
1 or 2 fresh pineapples – remove skin and core
   or 2 large (425g) cans pineapple chunks in juice, drained
2–3 large, ripe comice pears
8 oz/225g fresh strawberries – buy small ones and leave whole

Prepare the fruit, cut into bite-size pieces or slices and mix in the serving bowl. Moisten with ¼–½ pint/150ml–300ml orange juice, pineapple juice from the canned pineapple, sweet white wine or a mixture of the three, with a dash of orange liqueur if liked – but do not add too much liquid. Cover and leave to chill and marinate until ready to serve. Dish thick cream or Greek yoghurt separately.

THICK CREAM OR GREEK YOGHURT

I would provide 3 pints/1.7 litres of double cream and two 250g tubs of Greek yoghurt for this number of people. Whip the cream until thick but not solid to make it go further, and serve in bowls or jugs with spoons or ladles. Decant Greek yoghurt into serving bowls too, possibly labelled to avoid disasters!

CHEESE BOARDS   *Prepare 2.*

Very easy to prepare and serve. Make up the boards in the morning and leave covered with cling film in a cool place until ready to put on the table.

Put several large slabs of your favourite cheeses on each board, to make a good selection of tastes and textures, without looking as if you're running a pretentious restaurant! Start with a nice piece of Cheddar, a piece of Red Leicester or Double Gloucester and some Caerphilly or Lancashire for contrast. Add a slab of creamy Brie or a small Camembert, a good piece of Stilton or your favourite Blue, and perhaps a piece of Creamy Walnut for those who like a mild flavour. Garnish the boards with a few grapes or watercress and serve with a box of 'mixed biscuits for cheese'.

4

CHRISTENING

Tea Party to serve 24 people

A real family occasion, so the menu must include food suitable for all the guests, who may range from toddlers and starving teenagers to sophisticated aunts and uncles and doting grandparents, some of whom may have travelled a long distance to attend and will be hungry by tea-time.

All the food can be assembled in the morning (most of the dishes can be pre-cooked and frozen) and left covered with cling film in the fridge or a cool place. As you'll probably be busy with the baby before you go to church, if you're lucky enough to have a capable granny, auntie or neighbour willing to help, make a list of what needs to be done in the kitchen and of what is completely ready to put on the table for when you all arrive home. Even if you haven't got a helper, it's a simple matter on your return from church to pop any food that needs heating through into the oven and to put the rest onto the prepared serving table.

Many of the recipes for the Coming of Age party are suitable for this occasion too.

Open Rolls *** Club Sandwiches
Vol au Vents (page 29) *** Savoury Tartlets
Cheese Scones with Cream Cheese Spread
Cheese d'Artois (page 32) *** Savoury Sausage Jalousie
Devon Cream Scones *** Little Iced Fancies
Viennese Piped Biscuits
Sticky Gingerbread Slices
Nutty Strawberry Shortcake
Christening Cake

Tea *** Coffee *** Fruit Squash *** Fizzy Drinks
Wine *** Beers *** Spirits
Champagne

CHECK LISTS

THE MONTH BEFORE
Make and Freeze: Vol au Vents, Savoury Tartlets, Cheese d'Artois, Savoury Sausage Jalousie, Cheese Scones, Devon Cream Scones, Sticky Gingerbread, Viennese Biscuits, Little Iced Fancies and Nutty Strawberry Shortcake.

Make/Buy and Store: Christening Cake. Check your table linen and buy plenty of paper napkins. Arrange to borrow china, cutlery and an extra kettle if necessary. Buy or order soft and alcoholic drinks. Buy and freeze bread and rolls if there's room in your freezer. Buy long-life cream and store in the fridge. Buy butter (you need a lot!) or low fat spreads.

THE DAY BEFORE
Buy: Bread and rolls if not pre-frozen, and fresh cream.

Prepare the fillings and toppings for sandwiches, store them in the fridge, and make sauces and fillings for Vol au Vents if not pre-frozen. Take all the frozen goodies from the freezer and defrost. Set the buffet table if possible and prepare the table decorations.

ON THE DAY
Prepare, cover and store sandwiches and rolls. Fill Vol au Vent

cases, put them on baking trays ready to warm. Put Savoury Tartlets, Cheese d'Artois and Savoury Sausage Jalousie ready to warm. Spread Cheese Scones with cheesy spread and dish out. Whip the cream for scones and shortcakes, assemble Devon Scones or serve with jam and cream separately. Dish out the Gingerbread and Viennese Biscuits. Cut the Tray Bake Cake into squares, decorate and arrange on a serving dish. Assemble and dish the Strawberry Shortcake, keep in the fridge until needed. Put kettles and teapots ready for 'instant cuppas' when you get home.

If possible, arrange for a friend or neighbour to begin to warm the Vol au Vents, etc., ready for your return from church, or pre-set the oven timer to heat the oven ready for your return, and put the pastry dishes into the oven while everyone is arriving home.

OPEN ROLLS   *12 rolls – 24 halves.*

A more substantial snack, useful if you have teenagers to feed, or people who may have missed lunch in order to arrive on time.

Prepare the toppings the day before, and store in the fridge. Split the rolls in half and butter each half (allow 1 × 250g packet butter). Top with the chosen toppings (see opposite), decorate attractively, arrange on a serving dish, and cover with cling film until needed.

CLUB SANDWICHES
12 'rounds' of triple decker sandwiches.

Mix and match brown and white bread, and fill with contrasting fillings to look pretty. Leave crusts on or off according to the ages and appetites of your guests. Use one brown or granary loaf and one white thin sliced loaf, and butter the appropriate number of slices using one pack of softened butter (removing the crusts before spreading). Assemble the slices in threes, and make into triple deck sandwiches, using a good variety of fillings. Cut into triangles or fingers and arrange upright on a serving plate so that the fillings show. Garnish with cress, and cover with cling film until needed.

TOPPINGS AND FILLINGS
Egg Mayonnaise: See page 95.

Egg and Smoked Salmon: Add 4 oz/100g chopped smoked salmon to a 4 egg quantity of egg mayonnaise, and season with lemon juice.

Cold Meats: Ham with mustard, ox tongue with chutney, garlic sausage and salami, roast beef with horseradish sauce, chicken or turkey with cranberry sauce.

Tuna or Salmon: Drain the canned fish. Mash and season with vinegar or mayonnaise, salt and pepper. Good with cucumber.

Crab Meat: Available fresh or canned; it's nice with watercress.

Prawns: Mix 8 oz/225g fresh or defrosted prawns with the same amount of cream cheese or drained cottage cheese, or mix with egg mayonnaise.

Cheese: 8 oz/225g grated Cheddar cheese mixed with 2–3 tblsp chutney or mayonnaise.

Cottage Cheese: Available in various flavours: plain, or with pineapple, cucumber, or prawns. Drain well before use.

Cream Cheese: A nice thick layer on its own or with fish or salads.

Salads: Sliced tomatoes, washed shredded lettuce (mixed sorts look attractive), sliced cucumber, cress, watercress.

SAVOURY TARTLETS

Makes 24.

Individual quiches, cooked and frozen in advance. Make some of each filling.

Preparation and cooking time: 50–60 minutes.

1 lb/500g flour quantity shortcrust pastry or
** 2 × 13 oz/350g packs frozen shortcrust pastry – defrosted**

Heat the oven at 190°C/375°F/gas 5–6/fan 180°C. Roll out the pastry, cut into 3″/7.5cm circles and line 24 patty tins. Prick the pastry well and bake for about 10 minutes until crisp and very pale golden (prick any bubbles if the pastry begins to rise). Remove from the oven and leave in the tins. Reduce the oven to 180°C/350°F/gas 4–5/fan 170°C.

QUICHE LORRAINE FILLING

Fills 12 cases.

2 tsp oil for frying
1 medium onion – very finely chopped
4 oz/100g bacon – rind removed and chopped
1 egg – beaten
¼ pint/150ml double cream
Handful fresh chives or parsley – washed and snipped
Salt and pepper

Heat the oil in a pan over a moderate heat, and fry the onion and bacon for 4–5 minutes until softened. Drain and divide between the pastry cases. Mix the beaten egg, cream, herbs and seasoning and pour over the onion mixture.

CHEESE AND ASPARAGUS FILLING

Fills 12 cases.

1 × 300g can asparagus tips – drained
4 oz/100g mature Cheddar cheese – grated
1 egg – beaten
¼ pint/150ml double cream
Salt and black pepper

Divide the asparagus tips between the pastry cases and sprinkle the cheese on top. Mix the egg, cream and seasoning and pour over the filling.

To bake tartlets: Cook in the moderate oven (180°C/350°F/gas 4–5/fan 170°C) for 15–20 minutes until the filling is set. Remove carefully from the tins, cool and freeze, or serve at once.

To serve: Defrost and reheat in a moderate oven as before for 10–15 minutes. Dish and serve warm if possible.

CHEESE SCONES WITH CREAM CHEESE SPREAD
Makes 12–15 (24–30 halves).

Quick to make and they freeze well.

Preparation and cooking time: 30–35 minutes.

1 lb/450g self-raising flour
2 tsp baking powder
1 level tsp salt
1 level tsp dry mustard powder
4 oz/100g margarine
6 oz/150g mature Cheddar cheese – grated
Approx. ½ pint/275ml milk to mix

Heat the oven at 200°C/400°F/gas 6–7/fan 190°C. Sieve the dry ingredients into a bowl, rub in the margarine, add the cheese and mix to a stiff dough with milk. Turn onto a floured board and press out lightly to about 1″/2.5cm thick. Cut into rounds with a 2″/5cm cutter, re-rolling the trimmings until all the dough is used. Pat into good round shapes with a knife, bake in the hot oven for 10–15 minutes until risen and golden. Cool on a wire tray and freeze as soon as possible to keep fresh.

To serve: Defrost. Cut the scones into halves. Using one 250g pack of butter and a 200g pack of cheese spread, top the halved scones and serve garnished with watercress.

SAVOURY SAUSAGE JALOUSIE   *Makes 24 fingers.*

A quick, tasty variation on the sausage roll theme.

Preparation and cooking time: 1 hour.

1 onion – peeled and very finely chopped, or grated
1 lb/454g sausage meat or skinned sausages
1 tsp mixed herbs
1 egg – beaten
Salt and pepper
1 medium cooking apple – peeled, cored and thinly sliced
1 × 1 lb/454g pack puff pastry – thawed
Milk for brushing

Heat the oven at 210°C/410°F/gas 6–7/fan 200°C. Use a fork to mix together the chopped onion, sausage meat, herbs, egg and seasoning.

Roll out three-quarters of the pastry into an oblong 12″ × 8″/ 30cm × 20cm and put onto a baking tray. Spread the sausage mixture over the pastry almost to the edges, and arrange the apple slices neatly on top. Roll out the reserved pastry, cut into ½″/1cm strips and arrange in a trellis over the apple, damping the edges with water and pressing them tightly together.

Brush the pastry with milk and bake in the hot oven for 10 minutes. Then reduce the heat to 180°C/350°F/gas 4–5/fan 170°C for a further 20–30 minutes until the sausage is cooked. Cool and freeze, or serve.

To serve: Defrost thoroughly. Warm through in the moderate oven as above (180°C/350°F/gas 4–5/fan 170°C) for 10–15 minutes. Cut into fingers and arrange on a serving dish, or leave whole for people to help themselves.

DEVON CREAM SCONES
Makes 12–15 (24–30 halves).

Yummy – what more can I say!

Preparation and cooking time: 30–35 minutes.

1 lb/450g self-raising flour
2 tsp baking powder
4 oz/100g margarine
4 oz/100g sugar
4 oz/100g washed dried fruit (optional)
Approx. ½ pint/275ml milk

Make, bake and freeze as for Cheese Scones (see page 55), omitting the salt, mustard and cheese, but adding the sugar and dried fruit.

To serve: Use one 250g pack of butter, a 1 lb/450g jar of good strawberry jam and ½ pint/275ml double cream, stiffly whipped, or Devon cream if you can get it. Defrost the scones, cut them in half and top generously; if you come from Devon, you'll omit the butter and put a generous dollop of cream topped with jam. For a D.I.Y. job, put the scones in a basket, with a dish of butter and bowls of cream and jam nearby.

LITTLE ICED FANCIES *Makes 24.*

Use the recipe for Tray Bakes on page 11 and make one or two batches according to the number of youngsters at the party. Open freeze the iced cake slabs whole, then overwrap and store in the freezer.

To serve: Defrost on the day and cut into 24 squares. Decorate the individual cakes with smarties, jelly babies, tiny soft sweets, chocolate or multi-coloured 'sprinkles', glacé cherries, angelica, etc., or leave plain. Do not put coloured decorations on until the cakes are fully thawed or the colours may run. Put the decorated fancies into paper cases and serve.

VIENNESE PIPED BISCUITS

Makes 24–30.

These biscuits look most attractive on the tea table.

Preparation and cooking time: 25 minutes
plus 15 minutes chilling time.

8 oz/225g softened butter
2 oz/50g icing sugar – sieved
10 oz/275g plain flour – sieved

For decoration
4 oz/100g cooking chocolate
Few glacé cherries

Heat the oven at 180°C/350°F/gas 4–5/fan 170°C. Cream the fat and sugar well, then gradually beat in the flour. Put into a forcing bag with a ½″/1cm star tube and pipe 2″/5cm fingers and stars onto two greased baking trays. Top the stars with a piece of glacé cherry. Leave to chill in the fridge for 15 minutes, then bake in the moderate oven for 10–15 minutes until a pale biscuit colour. Cool completely on a wire tray.

When quite cold, melt the chocolate in a basin (over hot water or in the microwave), and coat the ends of the finger biscuits by dipping them into the chocolate and leaving to set over the edges of the wire tray. When set and dry, open freeze and then store in a plastic box.

To serve: Defrost. Dust the cherry stars with a little sieved icing sugar, and arrange the stars and fingers on a serving plate.

STICKY GINGERBREAD SLICES
Makes 2 loaves; with 10–12 slices each.

Very cheap to make, but very popular, so you may need to make double quantity.

Preparation and cooking time: 1 hour 15 minutes.

10 oz/275g plain flour
2 level tsp bicarbonate of soda
2 heaped tsp ground ginger
6 oz/150g golden syrup
2 oz/50g lard or margarine
2 oz/50g white or brown sugar
10 tblsp milk
2 oz/50g stem ginger (optional) – finely chopped

Heat the oven at 150°C/300°F/gas 2–3/fan 140°C. Grease and line two 1 lb/450g or 6″/15cm square cake tins. Sieve the flour, bicarbonate of soda and ginger into a bowl. Melt the syrup, fat and sugar in a pan over a low heat, then beat into the flour mixture, adding the milk to make a thick batter. Beat well, stir in the chopped ginger if used, pour into the tins and bake for 50–60 minutes until well risen and just firm to the touch.

Cool slightly, remove from the tins and cool completely on a wire tray. Freeze until needed.

To serve: Defrost completely. Cut into thick slices and spread with butter if liked. Put onto a serving dish and cover with cling film until needed.

NUTTY STRAWBERRY SHORTCAKE
Serves 10–12, so make 2 or 3.

The shortcake rounds can be made in advance and frozen or stored for a few days in an airtight tin, just leaving the cake to be assembled before serving. If fresh strawberries are not available, use fresh or frozen raspberries.

Preparation time: 45–55 minutes. Assembly time: 10–15 minutes.

4 oz/100g plain flour ⎫ **or 6 oz/175g**
2 oz/50g cornflour or rice flour ⎬ **plain flour**
2 oz/50g castor sugar
4 oz/100g butter
4 oz/100g ground nuts – mixed, hazelnuts or walnuts – see page 15
Filling
1 pint/600ml double cream
1–2 tblsp icing sugar
1 lb/454g fresh strawberries

Heat the oven at 160°C/325°F/gas 3–4/fan 150°C. Grease and line two 9″/22.5cm sandwich tins with baking parchment. Put the flours and sugar into a bowl, rub in the butter and stir in the ground nuts. Knead together into a stiff ball of dough. Divide into 2 pieces and flatten into the tins. Flute the edges with thumb and finger and prick all over. Bake for 25–30 minutes until lightly biscuit-coloured. Leave to cool in the tins for 5 minutes, then carefully tip onto wire trays, remove the parchment and cool completely. When cold, store in an airtight container or freeze.

To assemble: Do not assemble too early or the shortcake will go soggy. Defrost the shortcakes if frozen. Whip the cream with icing sugar to taste until stiff. Reserve a few strawberries for decoration, slice the rest of the berries and fold them into the whipped cream. Put one shortcake round onto a serving plate, cover with half the fruit cream, carefully top with the other round and cover with the remaining cream. Decorate with the reserved strawberries and keep cool until ready to serve.

5
SILVER WEDDING

Hot Fork Buffet to serve 24 people

This meal can be prepared in advance, leaving only final reheating to the last minute. Try out pans and dishes beforehand when cooking for large numbers, making sure that everything can be fitted into oven, microwave, or on top of the stove at the appropriate time as needed – you may need to 'borrow' space in a neighbour's cooker if you can't fit everything into your own.

Buffet food must be easy to eat, but also try and organise tables and chairs for as many people as possible, since that is far more comfortable than trying to balance everything on your knee.

Each main course recipe here feeds 12 people, as that is about the maximum amount that can be cooked in your largest casserole dishes. Depending on how many you are entertaining, choose any number of main course dishes, but remember that most people will want a taste of everything, so make sure there's enough to go round.

Mark's Mixed Pepper Starter
Bread Rolls * Butter**

Spicy Prawns
Aubergine Bake
Cider and Walnut Chicken
Tiny New Potatoes * Fresh French Beans**
Savoury Rice
Mushrooms à la Greque
Mixed Green Salad (double the ingredients given on page 9)
French Dressing (double the quantity made on page 10)

Fresh Pineapple Sorbet
Chocolate Roulade
Creamy Blackberry Mousse
Fresh Cream

CHECK LISTS

THE MONTH BEFORE
Make and Freeze: Cider and Walnut Chicken, sauce for Spicy
Prawns, Aubergine Bake, Savoury Rice, Pineapple Sorbet,
Chocolate Roulade and Creamy Blackberry Mousse.

Buy and Freeze: Prawns for Spicy Prawns and bread rolls.
Try out your arrangements for heating all the hot dishes before
serving; make sure you've got enough oven or hob space, and
enough space for keeping the cooked food warm until needed.
Check you've got enough table linen, plates, dishes and cutlery,
and buy paper napkins if necessary.

THE WEEK BEFORE
Buy and Store: Peppers, salad stuff (including ingredients for
the French dressing), mushrooms, butter, new potatoes and
French beans.

THE DAY BEFORE
Make/Buy and Refrigerate: Mixed Pepper Starter, Mushrooms
à la Greque, the French dressing and any main dish not already
in the freezer. Buy cream. Wash new potatoes and store in a
cool place; wash the salad vegetables and store in the fridge; top

and tail the French beans and store in the fridge.

Assemble the china, cutlery and glasses, and set the buffet table if possible. Remove the frozen main courses and the Savoury Rice from the freezer and leave to defrost.

ON THE DAY

Defrost the prawns, add to the defrosted prepared sauce and store in the fridge until ready to heat and serve. Defrost the Chocolate Roulade and store in a cool place. Defrost, dish and garnish the Blackberry Mousse, then store in the fridge. Put the Pineapple Sorbet at the top of the freezer ready to defrost later when needed. Defrost the bread rolls. Make the Green Salad and serve in two large salad bowls, accompanied by the French dressing in separate bowls or jugs. Dish the Pepper Starter.

Heat all the main courses, cook and dish the potatoes, reheat the Savoury Rice, and heat the Mushrooms à la Greque or serve cold.

Cook the beans and keep everything warm while eating the starter.

Serve the main course. Put the Pineapple Sorbet to soften in the fridge while eating the main course.

Serve the desserts.

MARK'S MIXED PEPPER SALAD
Serves 12; if you prefer, make two lots.

Our chalet chef kindly gave me this recipe after we enjoyed it during a ski trip. It's ideal for preparing in advance; in fact, it's best made the day before and left in the fridge to marinate and absorb the flavours – it just needs dishing out on the day.

Preparation and cooking time: 1 hour, plus 24 hours marinating.

6 large sweet peppers – red, green, yellow

Marinade
½ pint/300ml good olive oil
¼ pint/150ml wine vinegar
2 cloves garlic – peeled and crushed
1 bay leaf
Pinch oregano
Salt, black pepper

Bunch parsley to garnish – chopped

Heat the oven at 200°C/400°F/gas 6–7/fan 190°C. Wash the peppers, halve them longways and remove the seeds. Place them skinside down on an oiled roasting tin and roast in the hot oven for 30 minutes. Turn the peppers over and roast for a further 15 minutes. Remove from the oven and cool.

Peel the peppers; the skins should be blistered and come away easily to be discarded. Slice the peppers into a dish. Mix the marinade, pour over the peppers, cover and refrigerate for 24 hours, occasionally stirring carefully.

To serve: Remove from the fridge 1–2 hours before serving and bring back to room temperature. Serve, with the marinade, on a large platter or on individual plates, garnished with plenty of chopped parsley.

SPICY PRAWNS
Serves 12; if you prefer, make two lots.

The sauce can be cooked in advance and frozen, then defrosted and the prawns added on the day.

Preparation and cooking time: 45–50 minutes.

3 tblsp cooking oil
4–5 cloves garlic – peeled and crushed
3 large onions – peeled and finely chopped
3 tblsp garam masala
3 × 400g cans chopped tomatoes
1 tblsp tomato purée or chopped, sun-dried tomatoes
2½ lb/1.25kg frozen prawns
Garnish
Few lemon slices
Little chopped parsley

Heat the oil in a large, heavy pan over a moderate heat. Add the garlic and onion, and fry gently for 8–10 minutes until softened but not browned. Add the garam masala and stir well. Pour in the chopped tomatoes, add the tomato purée or sun-dried tomatoes, stir well and simmer without a lid for about 30 minutes, stirring occasionally, until you have a lovely thick 'tomatoey' sauce. Either finish the dish (as below) and serve, or cool the sauce and freeze in a plastic box.

To serve: Defrost the sauce. Defrost and drain the prawns well, patting off excess moisture with kitchen paper. Put the sauce into a pan, stir in the prawns and bring slowly to the boil. Then simmer very gently for just a few minutes to heat right through – do not overcook or the prawns will toughen, as they are already cooked before freezing. Pour into a hot serving dish or into a ring of savoury rice (see page 69), and garnish with lemon slices and a little chopped parsley.

AUBERGINE BAKE
Serves 12; if you prefer, make two lots.

If you're providing this dish for your vegetarian guests, make sure you have plenty of it since lots of your other guests will also want 'a taste' with their chicken or fish.

Preparation and cooking time: 1½ hours.

4 tblsp cooking oil
3 large onions – peeled and chopped
4–6 cloves garlic – peeled and crushed
2 × 440g cans cooked beans (barlotti, cannellini or haricot)
1 × 800g can tomatoes – chopped a bit
2 tsp mixed herbs
3 tblsp tomato purée
Salt and pepper
2 tsp sugar
6 even-sized aubergines
8 oz/225g strong Cheddar cheese – grated
3 tblsp grated Parmesan cheese
Watercress to garnish

Heat the oil in a large frying pan, and fry the chopped onion and garlic gently until soft but not browned. Add the drained beans, chopped tomatoes, herbs, tomato purée, salt, pepper and sugar. Wash the aubergines, cut them in half lengthways, scoop out the flesh (cut round the edges with a vegetable knife, cut criss-cross across the middle and scoop out ½"/1cm cubes) and add to the tomato mixture in the pan. Simmer gently for 15–20 minutes, stirring occasionally.

Blanch the aubergine shells in a big pan of boiling water for 3–4 minutes, drain well and arrange in one or two large ovenproof dishes (buy foil dishes if you don't have suitable dishes) and fill the shells with the tomato mixture (it will probably fill the dish and may spill over). Mix the cheeses and sprinkle over the top. Either bake and serve (as below), or freeze until needed.

To bake and serve: Defrost. Bake covered with foil in a hot oven (200°C/400°F/gas 6–7/fan 190°C) for 20 minutes. Remove the foil and bake for a further 15–20 minutes until the top is crispy and golden. Garnish with watercress and serve hot.

CIDER AND WALNUT CHICKEN
Serves 12; if you prefer, make two lots.

A creamy chicken dish, made with boneless chicken breasts for easy eating. Cut the pieces in half so that people can take a small amount if they wish to taste all the dishes on offer.

Preparation and cooking time: 1½–1¾ hours.

12–18 (according to size) boneless chicken breasts – halved
3 tblsp oil for frying
4 large onions – peeled and thinly chopped
2 large cooking apples – peeled and sliced
8 oz/225g streaky bacon rashers – rind removed and sliced
2 tblsp cornflour
½ pint/300ml cider
4 oz/100g walnut pieces (see page 15)
2 tsp mixed herbs
1 pint/600ml chicken stock (use 2–3 stock cubes)
Salt and pepper
Garnish
2 oz/50g walnut halves
¼ pint/150ml double cream or yoghurt

Heat the oven at 180°C/350°F/gas 4–5/fan 170°C. Heat the oil in a large frying pan and fry the halved chicken breasts on both sides until lightly browned. Remove and put into a large casserole dish.

Fry the onion, apple and bacon for 4–5 minutes until softened, then add to the chicken. Mix the cornflour to a runny paste with a little cider, pour the rest of the cider into the frying pan and scrape up all the chicken juices and pour over the chicken in the casserole, adding the walnut pieces and herbs. Stir the cornflour paste into the chicken stock, stir well and add to the casserole. Season with salt and pepper, cover and cook in the moderate oven for approximately 45 minutes until the sauce has thickened and the chicken is cooked. Garnish and serve, or cool and freeze in a plastic container.

To serve: Defrost thoroughly. Pour into a casserole dish and reheat in a moderate oven (180°C/350°F/gas 4–5/fan 170°C) for 20–30 minutes until cooked right through, not just warmed. Sprinkle with walnut halves and swirl with cream or yoghurt. Serve hot.

TINY NEW POTATOES

If potatoes are the only accompaniments to the main course, allow 12 lb/5.5kg for generous helpings for 24 people. But if you're also serving Savoury Rice, 8 lb/3.5kg should be plenty.

The potatoes can be washed and lightly scrubbed the day before and left in a cool place until needed (in cold water if you've removed much skin).

To cook and serve: Cook in boiling, salted water, with some sprigs of fresh mint if possible, for 10–15 minutes, until just soft (do not overcook). Drain thoroughly, return to the pan, and toss in a little butter, then tip into serving dishes and keep warm, garnishing with fresh mint before serving.

FRESH FRENCH BEANS

Allow 4 lb/1.75kg fresh beans (you can use the same amount of frozen beans if fresh are not available). Top and tail the day before and store in a polythene bag in the fridge. Cook in a little boiling, salted water for 3–4 minutes, just before serving the starter. Drain well, toss in a little butter, dish and keep warm until needed.

SAVOURY RICE   *Serves 12; if you prefer, make two lots.*

The rice can be prepared in advance, frozen and reheated before serving, or cooked on the day. It is quite a substantial dish in its own right. When freezing and reheating rice, it should be cooked and frozen as quickly as possible, and heated right through when re-heating.

Preparation and cooking time: 45 minutes for white rice
1 hour for brown rice.

1½ lb/750g long grain white or brown rice – washed
8 oz/225g frozen mixed vegetables
4 oz/100g frozen peas
1 × 300g can sweetcorn – drained
2 tblsp turmeric
Salt and black pepper
Parsley or prawns (see page 65) to garnish

Cook the chosen rice in boiling, salted water as instructed on the packet. Drain well and tip into a large bowl. Put the frozen vegetables into a pan with the minimum of boiling water and bring to the boil (do not overcook), drain and add to the rice. Drain the sweetcorn and stir into the mixture, and stir in the turmeric, mixing well to give an even yellow colour. Season well, and use at once, or cool and freeze in a covered plastic box.

To serve: Defrost the rice either overnight or in the morning. Heat the oven at 150°C/300°F/gas 2–3/fan 140°C. Tip the rice mixture into a greased ovenproof dish, cover with foil and heat for 20–30 minutes, stirring occasionally, until hot. Serve garnished with parsley or tip onto a large platter, form into a deep ring and fill with Spicy Prawns (see page 65).

MUSHROOMS À LA GRECQUE (ish!)
Serves 12; if you prefer, make two lots.

Can be served hot or cold according to taste and how much oven space you have available at the last minute. The dish can be prepared and cooked the day before most successfully, but I prefer not to freeze mushrooms as I think it makes them taste mushy.

Preparation and cooking time: 1–1¼ hours.

2–2¼ lb/1kg medium-sized mushrooms – washed and sliced
4 tblsp oil
4 medium-sized onions – peeled and very thinly sliced
¼ pint/150ml dry white wine
4 tblsp tomato purée
1 pint/600ml vegetable stock – use 2 vegetable stock cubes
Salt and black pepper
½ tsp each of oregano and marjoram
Shake paprika and chopped parsley to garnish

Heat the oven at 160°C/325°F/gas 3–4/fan 150°C. Lightly blanch the sliced mushrooms in a large pan of boiling water, drain well and pour into an ovenproof dish.

Heat the oil in a pan over a medium heat and fry the onion gently for 5 minutes until soft but not brown, and add to the mushrooms. Swill the wine round with the juices in the pan and pour over the mushrooms. Drizzle the tomato purée over the vegetables, cover with the stock and season with salt, pepper and herbs. Cover with a foil lid and bake for about 45 minutes until the vegetables are cooked. Serve or store in the fridge.

To serve: Serve cold at room temperature (allow 1–2 hours out of the fridge), or reheat in a moderate oven (160°C/325°F/gas 3–4/fan 150°C) for 20–30 minutes. Garnish with a shake of paprika and chopped parsley.

FRESH PINEAPPLE SORBET
Serves 12 big or 24 small helpings.

A very pretty and eye-catching dessert which is made in advance and frozen – but just remember to take it out of the freezer to soften before serving. You will need a liquidiser or food processor for this recipe.

Preparation and cooking time: 30 minutes plus freezing time.

8 oz/225g granulated sugar
1 pint/600ml water
2 large ripe fresh pineapples – washed and dried
4 egg whites
1–2 packets 'posh' wafers

Make the sugar syrup: Put the sugar and water into a large, heavy pan over a moderate heat and cook slowly until all the sugar has dissolved, stirring well. Bring to the boil and bubble gently (don't let it boil over) for 10–15 minutes, until the liquid is thick and syrupy. Leave to cool.

Cut each pineapple in half lengthways, scoop out the flesh and purée in a liquidiser or processor. Pour into a bowl, add the cooled syrup and mix well. Pour into freezer trays or a shallow plastic box and freeze until mushy but not hard.

Tip the sorbet into a bowl and beat with a mixer until soft. Beat the egg whites until stiff and fold into the soft pineapple mixture. Spoon the mixture into the pineapple shells and open freeze until hard. Wrap each fruit separately in plastic film, put into a freezer bag and store in the freezer until needed.

To serve: Unwrap each pineapple half, put onto a serving dish and stand in the fridge for 30 minutes before serving, accompanied with posh sugar wafers.

CHOCOLATE ROULADE
Serves 8–10; make 2 or 3 as it's always very popular!

A special, rich dessert, but this recipe is easy to make and tastes marvellous.

Preparation and cooking time: 1 hour, plus cooling time.

6 large eggs – separated
8 oz/225g castor sugar
½ tsp vanilla essence
2 oz/50g cocoa – sieved
Filling and Decoration
8 oz/225g plain cooking chocolate
1½ oz/35g unsalted butter
1 pint/600ml double cream

Heat the oven at 180°C/350°F/gas 4–5/fan 170°C. Line a large (13″ × 8½″/33cm × 21cm) Swiss roll tin with baking parchment. Whip the egg yolks, sugar and vanilla until very thick and creamy and fold in the sieved cocoa. Beat the egg whites until stiff and fold carefully into the mixture. Pour into the lined tin, spread evenly and bake for about 20 minutes (do not open the oven door while the cake is rising) until well risen, set and just firm to the touch.

Grease a sheet of baking parchment and sprinkle with castor sugar. Remove the cake from the oven, leave to cool slightly, then turn out onto the prepared paper and leave to cool. Trim off any crisp edges of cake.

Make the filling: Melt the chocolate (either in a bowl over hot water or in the microwave), and beat the butter into the melted chocolate. Whip the cream until stiff. Spread the chocolate over the cake and cover with a thick layer of the cream, reserving some for decoration. Roll up the roulade, taking care not to squidge the cream out of the sides. Decorate with piped swirls of whipped cream and open freeze.

To serve: Defrost on the day, put on a serving plate and keep cool until ready to serve.

CREAMY BLACKBERRY MOUSSE
Serves 12 so make 2.

This dessert can be assembled on the day from previously prepared fruit purée, or made completely and frozen in advance. You'll need a liquidiser or processor.

Preparation and cooking time: 20 minutes, plus cooling and setting or freezing time.

2 lb/1kg blackberries – washed and drained
8 oz/225g sugar (or to taste)
1 packet/½ oz/14g gelatine or agar-agar (vegetarian gelatine)
4 egg whites
½ pint/300ml double cream

Cook the blackberries in a large pan, with 1–2 tblsp water, until soft (about 5–10 minutes). Liquidise or process the cooked fruit and sieve to give a velvety purée. Sweeten to taste and leave to cool.

Dissolve the gelatine or agar-agar as instructed on the packet and add to the fruit, stirring well. Whip the egg whites until stiff and whip the cream until thick but not solid, then fold both into the fruit. Freeze in a plastic box or pour into a serving dish and leave to set.

To serve: Defrost on the day and pour gently into a serving dish or individual glasses. Decorate with a few fresh berries if available and refrigerate until ready to serve.

FRESH CREAM

The desserts are so rich that you don't really need any extra cream, but there's always somebody (probably my husband!) who feels cheated if there isn't more cream to slosh on top, so I would whip 1 pint/600ml double cream until thick and serve it in a large bowl or jug with the desserts.

6

GOLDEN WEDDING

Hot Sit-Down Dinner to serve 12 people

This is a more extravagant menu, suitable for a very special occasion, when you are possibly catering for smaller numbers than in the previous chapters. Older people often prefer a luxury version of familiar dishes and are more comfortable with a sit-down meal than a buffet, even if it does mean a bit of a squeeze around the dining table or setting up an extra table for some of the guests. Most of the basic preparations can be done in advance, just leaving the final touches to do on the day.

**Smoked Salmon Cornets with Prawns and
Lemon Mayonnaise
Granary Bread and Butter**

**Boeuf en Croûte
Dauphine Potatoes
Courgette Ratatouille *** Mange Tout with Petit Pois
'Green' Green Salad (page 9) *** French Dressing (page 10)**

**Sugary Apple Cake with Thick Cream
Cheese and Biscuits
Coffee and Mints**

CHECK LISTS

THE MONTH BEFORE

Make and Freeze: Boeuf en Croûte, Courgette Ratatouille, Sugary Apple Cake.

Buy and Freeze/Store: Smoked Salmon, prawns, granary bread, mange tout, petit pois. Buy or order alcoholic and soft drinks. Check your table linen and buy paper napkins if necessary. Buy and store biscuits for cheese.

THE DAY BEFORE

Buy: Fresh vegetables, bread if not pre-frozen, and cheeses. Make Lemon Mayonnaise and French dressing and refrigerate. Peel and slice the potatoes, store in cold water in a cool place. Grate the cheese for the scalloped potatoes. Prepare the Courgette Ratatouille (if not pre-frozen) and store in the fridge. Top and tail fresh petit pois and store in the fridge. Wash and drain lettuce, salad vegetables, celery or grapes for the cheese board and store in the fridge.

THE EVENING BEFORE

Set the table if possible, including any side-plates for the salad if you've got room on the table! Put out the serving dishes and make the table decorations. Leave the smoked salmon and Boeuf en Croûte to defrost in the fridge overnight.

ON THE DAY

Defrost the Apple Cake and granary bread. Defrost the prawns and store in the fridge. Prepare the Green Salad, cover with cling film and keep cool. Prepare the starters and store in the fridge. (You may have to make them at the last minute if you're short of fridge space.) Dish the bread and butter. Put the Apple Cake on an ovenproof serving dish ready to warm, whip and dish the cream and store in the fridge. Prepare the cheese board, leaving the cheeses out of the fridge to 'come to'. Take the French dressing from the fridge and toss the salad at the last minute or serve the dressing separately in a small sauce boat.

Timing the main course to be ready to eat when required, cook the Dauphine Potatoes and later the Boeuf en Croûte. Heat the Courgette Ratatouille and keep warm. Cook the peas and mange tout at the last minute and keep warm. Put the plates to warm and keep the main course dishes warm while eating the starter – and then don't forget to serve the salad which is in a cool place. Put the Sugary Apple Cake to warm in the now empty oven while eating the main course, and put the kettle on ready for coffee.

SMOKED SALMON CORNETS WITH PRAWNS AND LEMON MAYONNAISE
Serves 12.

Gives a luxury start to the meal, quickly assembled on the day.

Preparation time: 20 minutes, plus time for making mayonnaise if home-made.

1½ lb/750g (24 slices) smoked salmon
1½ lb/750g large peeled prawns
1 cucumber – thinly sliced
1 pint/600ml mayonnaise (home-made, see page 10, or good shop-bought, mixed with juice of 1 lemon – 2–3 tblsp)
12 whole, unshelled prawns to garnish, if possible
Paprika pepper
3 lemons to garnish
2 granary French sticks or 1 large granary loaf
1 × 250g pack unsalted butter

Prepare 12 individual plates. Roll the smoked salmon slices into cornets and arrange two on each plate. Divide the prawns equally and put a pile on each plate, with some cucumber slices and a dollop of lemon mayonnaise. Garnish with the whole prawns and a shake of paprika on the mayonnaise. Refrigerate until ready to serve, accompanied with lemon wedges, granary bread and butter.

BOEUF EN CROÛTE   *Serves 6 generously, so make 2.*

A luxury version of roast beef to grace a very special occasion. Prepare it in advance and freeze uncooked.

Preparation and cooking time: 1½ hours
                                   plus 20–25 minutes on the day.

1½–1¾ lb/750g thick piece fillet steak
3 tblsp vegetable oil
2 onions – peeled and finely chopped
12 oz/350g mushrooms – washed and sliced
1 tsp mixed herbs
Small, bunch parsley – washed and snipped
Salt and pepper
1 × 1 lb/454g pack puff pastry – defrosted
Beaten egg or milk for brushing

Heat the oven at 200°C/400°F/gas 6–7/fan 190°C. Trim any gristly or fatty bits from the steak, brush with 1 tblsp oil, cover with foil and roast for 20–30 minutes, depending how rare you like your beef; this timing will give you a medium/medium rare steak when finished. Remove from the oven and leave to go cold, basting occasionally with the meat juices.

Meanwhile, heat 2 tblsp oil in a pan over a moderate heat, fry the chopped onion for 4–5 minutes until softened. Add the sliced mushrooms and continue to cook for 15–20 minutes, without a lid, stirring occasionally until the excess liquid has evaporated and you are left with a nice, thick, saucy mixture. Add the herbs and parsley and season to taste. Leave to cool.

Roll out the pastry into a rectangle, approximately 12″ × 10″/ 30cm × 25cm, big enough to wrap the meat in, and trim the edges neatly. Spoon the cold mushroom mixture along the pastry and carefully place the cooked fillet on top. Brush the edges of the pastry with beaten egg and fold the pastry over to make a neat oblong parcel, sealing all the edges. Roll out the pastry scraps, cut into leaf shapes and place decoratively on top of the croûte. Brush well with beaten egg or milk and lift carefully onto a baking sheet (use a fish slice), ready for baking, or open freeze and overwrap when frozen.

To serve: Defrost if pre-frozen. Bake in a pre-heated oven (210°C/410°F/gas 6–7/fan 200°C) for 20–25 minutes, until the pastry is well risen and golden brown. Remove to a warm carving dish and keep warm until ready to serve (do not leave standing for too long or the meat will overcook).

MANGE TOUT WITH PETIT POIS   *Serves 12.*

Mix fresh or frozen mange tout with frozen petit pois.

Preparation and cooking time: 5–15 minutes.

1½–2 lb/675–900g frozen petit pois
½ lb/225g fresh (topped and tailed) or frozen mange tout
Few sprigs fresh mint for cooking and garnishing
1 tsp sugar

Put the peas and prepared mange tout in a large saucepan, with a few sprigs mint, and half cover with boiling salted water. Bring back to the boil, boil for a few moments, remove from the heat, drain well and discard the mint. Pour into a serving dish, stir in the sugar, and keep warm until ready to serve, garnished with mint at the last minute.

DAUPHINE POTATOES   *Serves 6, so make 2 dishes.*

A deliciously rich form of scalloped potatoes. Not suitable for freezing but all the ingredients can be prepared the day before and quickly assembled and cooked on the day.

Preparation and cooking time: 2–2½ hours.

2 cloves garlic (optional) – peeled and chopped
Butter for greasing
3 lb/1.5kg potatoes – peeled and thinly sliced
8 oz/225g mature Cheddar cheese – grated
2 eggs – beaten
¾ pint/0.5 litre milk
Salt and black pepper
2 heaped tblsp grated Parmesan cheese

Rub the crushed garlic over the inside of a large ovenproof dish, approximately 5 pints/3 litres in size and 2–3″/5–7cm deep (if you haven't got suitable dishes, buy some foil ones). Grease the dish very well with butter.

Starting with potato, put alternate layers of potato and cheese into the dish until it is full, ending with a layer of cheese. Mix the beaten eggs, milk and seasoning and pour over the potatoes so that the mixture almost covers the layers. Sprinkle the top with grated Parmesan and put aside until ready to cook.

To cook: Heat the oven at 190°C/375°F/gas 5–6/fan 180°C and bake the dish in the hot oven for 1½–2 hours, until the potatoes are soft and the 'custard' is set. Cover lightly with foil and reduce the oven heat to 180°C/350°F/gas 4–5/fan 170°C if the top begins to get too brown. Time the potatoes to be ready with the Boeuf en Croûte; put them on a lower shelf for the last 20 minutes of cooking when you raise the oven temperature for the main course. Keep them warm until ready to serve.

COURGETTE RATATOUILLE   *Serves 12.*

A nice, bright vegetable dish, providing a sauce for the meat. It can be made the day before (the vegetables will taste even better having been left to marinate overnight) and served hot or cold. It can be pre-cooked and frozen, but the vegetables will not be quite so crisp.

Preparation and cooking time: 35–45 minutes.

3–4 tblsp olive oil
3 large onions – peeled and thinly sliced
3–4 cloves garlic (optional) – peeled and crushed
6 peppers (various colours) – de-seeded and sliced
2 lb/900g courgettes – trimmed and thickly sliced
2 × 425g cans tomatoes – drained and roughly chopped
Salt and black pepper
Handful chopped parsley to garnish

Heat the oil in a large pan over a moderate heat and fry the onion and garlic for 4–5 minutes until just softened but not browned. Add the peppers and continue to stir fry for a further 4–5 minutes until the peppers have just softened. Stir in the courgettes and mix gently, stirring in the chopped tomatoes and cooking gently for 5–10 minutes (do not overcook: the vegetables should be slightly crisp). Season to taste, cool and put aside in the fridge, or freeze.

To serve: Defrost the ratatouille and serve cold in a deep serving dish, or reheat gently in a pan on the hob for 10 minutes until piping hot, and pour into a warm serving dish. Garnish with plenty of chopped parsley.

SUGARY APPLE CAKE

Gives 8 slices, so make 2.

A change from apple pie, but not too different for those who may prefer familiar food. Can be made and frozen in advance, or will keep, covered, in the fridge for 3–4 days.

Preparation and cooking: 1½–1¾ hours.

3 oz/75g butter
4 oz/100g sugar
1 egg
Few drops vanilla or almond essence
4 oz/100g self-raising flour
1 level tsp baking powder
1 lb/450g cooking apples – peeled and thinly sliced
2 oz/50g sultanas – washed and drained
1–2 tblsp castor sugar for dredging

Heat the oven at 190°C/375°F/gas 5–6/fan 180°C. Grease very well an 8–8½"/20–21cm loose-based or spring-clip cake tin. Melt the butter gently until just liquid. Put the sugar, egg and essence into a mixing bowl, gradually pour in the melted butter and beat very well. Fold in the flour and baking powder and mix gently.

Spoon half the mixture into the tin, spread the apple on top and sprinkle with the sultanas. Cover with the rest of the cake mixture, smoothing it as evenly as possible, allowing for the lumpy apples underneath (it won't be very smooth, but that doesn't matter!). Sprinkle with 1–2 tblsp castor sugar and bake for about 1 hour, until slightly risen and golden, and the apple is cooked (reduce the heat to 180°C/350°F/gas 4–5/fan 170°C if the top seems to be getting too brown). Cool slightly, then remove from the tin upwards and lift the cake off the base with a fish slice (it will be rather fragile) and dredge with more castor sugar. Cool, wrap and freeze, or store in the fridge for 3–4 days.

To serve: Defrost completely. It can be served cold, but it's nicest warmed through in the still warm oven while you are eating the main course. Serve with 1 pint/600ml double cream, whipped until thick but not stiff, and poured into two serving bowls.

CHEESE AND BISCUITS

Serves 12.

Some people may prefer cheese instead of dessert, others may like to try both! As you are sitting at the table people will probably nibble cheese while chatting and enjoying themselves, especially as the cheese board will look so attractive. I would serve no more than three or four of my favourite kinds of cheese – possibly Stilton or Roquefort (depending on price!), Brie or Camembert, a mild Roulé of goat's cheese and a good Cheddar or Double Gloucester or other 'hard' cheese, which should provide something for everyone (after all, it's family and friends and you will know who likes what), allowing 1½–2oz/ 35–50g per person.

Serve with a box of mixed biscuits for cheese, a new packet of butter, and garnish the cheese board with a bunch of seedless grapes and a jug of celery.

COFFEE AND MINTS

Have the coffee things ready in the kitchen, remembering that there is usually at least one person who will prefer tea. Serve the drinks at the table or in the sitting room if you wish.

7

BONFIRE NIGHT

Hot Food to serve 24 people

Bonfire Night food, to be eaten safely outside around the bonfire or while watching the fireworks, needs to be fun, filling, warming and easy to eat in your hand without the need for elaborate plates and cutlery. It should also be easy to prepare in advance so that you can be outside watching the fireworks (and the children!) too.

Provide hot mulled wine, beer or wine for adults, and lots of soft drinks for everyone. Serve hot soup from a thermos, to drink from disposable cups, and lots of lovely traditional bonfire food. A stack of paper napkins and a plastic sack for the rubbish (paper cups and plates are safer than china and glass outdoors in the dark), and you're ready to light the bonfire.

Cream of Tomato Soup
Garlic Bread
Hot Dogs with Fried Onions
Roast Chicken Drumsticks

Foiled Jacket Potatoes with Choice of Fillings
Lancashire Parkin
Jane's Special Bonfire Toffee

Hot Mulled Wine *** Beer *** Wine *** Soft Drinks
Coffee or Tea

CHECK LISTS

THE MONTH BEFORE
Make/Buy and Freeze: Garlic Bread, French bread sticks, finger rolls, sausages, chicken drumsticks, Lancashire Parkin.

Buy and Store: Tins of soup, pickles, pineapple pieces, ketchup, mustards, sweetcorn, wines, beer, soft drinks, cooking foil, paper cups, plates and napkins. Arrange to borrow thermos flasks if necessary.

THE WEEK BEFORE
Make Lancashire Parkin, if not already made and frozen; store in an airtight tin. Buy butter, yoghurt, cheese (grate and store in the fridge), cream cheese, cottage cheese, cucumber and potatoes.

THE EVENING BEFORE
Scrub the jacket potatoes (but do not prick), and store in a cool place. Defrost the sausages and chicken overnight. Find the paper cups, plates and napkins. Collect together the serving dishes and cutlery.

ON THE DAY
Defrost the garlic bread, French sticks and bread rolls. Prepare the sausages and chicken for cooking, and store in the fridge. Make the Bonfire Toffee and store in an airtight tin. Prepare the fillings for the Jacket Potatoes, dish and store in the fridge. Prepare and cook the onions, and put aside to reheat before serving. Dish the Lancashire Parkin and cover with cling film. Prepare the mulled wine and put ready to heat. Prick and foil-wrap the potatoes. Place coffee- and tea-making equipment and plenty of mugs ready in the kitchen for later in the evening.

Timing the food to be ready and kept warm just before your

guests arrive, bake the potatoes, chicken drumsticks and sausages. Put the garlic bread ready for last-minute cooking. Heat the soup and pour into the thermos flasks. Re-heat the onions. Heat the mulled wine and taste to check it's just right.

There's the doorbell – ladle out the mulled wine and join your guests in the garden!

CREAM OF TOMATO SOUP
Serves 24 – allow 1–2 cups per person.

If you're a soup maker, then use your favourite recipe and make your own. However, soup for 24 is rather time-consuming, and children often prefer canned soup anyway. I've chosen a smooth soup so that there are no 'bits' in it, making it easy to drink from a cup. (Select any other smooth cream soup if you don't like tomato.)

6–8 × 800g cans tomato soup (or buy catering-size cans)

Heat the soup in advance, pour into hot thermos flasks, and serve with hot garlic bread or French bread and butter.

GARLIC BREAD   *Allow 4–6 loaves.*

I would leave 1 or 2 loaves plain for those who prefer it. Slice and spread each loaf with 4 oz/100g garlic butter (made by beating 2 cloves crushed garlic into the butter, with a handful of chopped parsley), wrap the loaf in foil and freeze. It may be necessary to cut the loaf in half before wrapping if it's too long to fit into the oven.

To serve: Defrost the loaves. Heat the oven at 200°C/400°F/ gas 6–7/fan 190°C and bake the foil-wrapped loaves for 5–10 minutes until the butter has melted and the bread is crisp and hot. Serve hot.

HOT DOGS
To serve 24 people – allow 1 or 2 per person.

Serve the sausages in soft finger rolls with plenty of ketchup and fried onions.

Preparation and cooking time: 25 minutes.

2–3 lb/1–1.5kg chipolata sausages
24–48 soft bread finger rolls
1 or 2 squeezy-type bottles of ketchup
English and French mustard

Prick the sausages, put into a large roasting tin and cook in a hot oven (200°C/400°F/gas 6–7/fan 190°C) for 20 minutes, turning to cook both sides. When nice and brown, remove the sausages and pile into a hot serving dish and keep warm until needed. If you have room in the oven, the bread rolls are lovely warmed through for a few minutes just before serving.

Either make up a big tray of hot dogs and serve accompanied with a big pan of fried onions and the inevitable ketchup, or put the lot on the table and let everyone make up their own concoctions!

FRIED ONIONS

Peel and slice thinly 3 lb/1.5kg onions. Heat 4 tblsp oil in a pan over a moderate heat, and fry the onions for 10–15 minutes stirring occasionally, until soft and golden. Put aside until needed.

To serve: Reheat the onions over a gentle heat, stirring well, and serve in the pan or in a hot serving dish to accompany the hot dogs.

ROAST CHICKEN DRUMSTICKS

To serve 24 people – allow 1 or 2 per person.

Buy the large packs from your supermarket (pre-frozen ones are usually cheaper than fresh or chilled).

24–48 chicken drumsticks, coated or plain as you like
3–4 tblsp cooking oil
2–3 tsp mixed herbs

Defrost the chicken thoroughly. Pour the oil into a large roasting tin, and arrange the drumsticks in the tin in one layer (you may need 2 tins). Sprinkle with the herbs and store in the fridge until ready to cook.

To cook and serve: Heat the oven at 200°C/400°F/gas 6–7/fan 190°C and roast the chicken for 20–25 minutes, turning to brown on all sides, until the juices run clear, not pink, when tested with a fork. Drain the drumsticks on kitchen paper, pile onto a serving dish and keep warm until needed.

FOILED JACKET POTATOES   *Allow 1 or 2 each.*

You may need to borrow space in a neighbour's oven, as you will also need oven space for last-minute cooking or heating of chicken, sausages, garlic bread and rolls. The spuds can be cooked in the bonfire, but unless you have expert campers to take care of this (and to keep the children away), it's probably safer and easier to cook them in the oven. The spuds are easier to serve and eat if foil-wrapped before cooking.

Preparation and cooking time: about 1½ hours.

Wash and scrub 36 or more medium-sized potatoes. Prick well and lightly wrap each potato in a square of foil. Bake in a hot oven (200°C/400°F/gas 6–7/fan 190°C) for 1¼–1½ hours according to size, timing them to be ready just before you want to serve them.

To serve: Using a cloth (they're jolly hot!) open out the foil of each potato, and cut a deep cross in the skin, so that the potato can easily be filled. Pile onto a serving dish and keep hot until needed.

FILLINGS FOR JACKET POTATOES
Provide a variety of fillings for people to help themselves.

  Butter: 3–4 250g packs.

  Grated Cheese: 1–1½ lb/450–750g Cheddar cheese, piled in bowls.

  Cream Cheese and/or Cottage Cheese: 2–4 250g cartons.

  Pickle or Chutney: 1–2 jars decanted into bowls. Use whatever mixture you have in the cupboard or looks good in the supermarket.

  Pineapple and Sweetcorn: 2–3 425g cans pineapple pieces drained and mixed with 2–3 330g cans drained sweetcorn.

  Tim's Tzatziki (as served by my eldest son in Greece when he was teaching windsurfing for the summer): Mix 1 pint/600ml Greek yoghurt with 1 finely diced cucumber. Season with 1–2 tblsp lemon juice, salt and black pepper. Serve in a bowl with a small ladle or spoon.

LANCASHIRE PARKIN
Cuts into 16 pieces, make 2 or 3.

Quick, easy and cheap. It should be made a week in advance and stored in a cake tin to allow the parkin to become really sticky, moist and utterly delicious.

Making and baking time: 1¼–1½ hours.

12 oz/350g medium oatmeal
6 oz/175g plain flour
½ tsp bicarbonate of soda
1 level tsp ground ginger
1 oz/25g soft brown sugar
4 oz/100g margarine or lard
6 oz/175g golden syrup
6 oz/175g black treacle
¼ pint/150ml (approximately) milk to mix

Heat the oven at 180°C/350°F/gas 4–5/fan 170°C. Grease and line the base of a 9″/22.5cm square tin. Put the oatmeal into a mixing bowl, sieve the flour into it, and add the bicarbonate of soda and ginger, and stir in the sugar.

Put the fat, syrup and treacle into a saucepan and heat very gently until the fat has melted and the mixture is warm, not hot. Pour onto the dry ingredients and mix well, beating in enough milk to make a thick, runny batter. Pour into the prepared tin and bake in the moderate oven for 20 minutes, then reduce the heat to 160°C/325°F/gas 3–4/fan 150°C for a further 40–50 minutes until the cake is a lovely brown colour and just firm to the touch.

Turn the cake carefully onto a wire rack and peel off the paper while hot. Leave to cool, then store in an airtight tin for a week before eating. Or wrap and freeze to defrost before serving. Serve cut into decent-sized chunks.

JANE'S SPECIAL BONFIRE TOFFEE
Make as much as you like!

A special Plymouth friend, who always makes this super toffee for our bonfire parties, gave me this recipe. It's very economical as the ingredients go an amazingly long way, but it soon goes sticky and soft, so it should be cooked and eaten on the same day. The children will enjoy watching the toffee liquid puff up to produce a big tin of toffee, but do supervise them carefully if you let them make it themselves, as liquid toffee is *very, very hot!*

Preparation and cooking time: 10 minutes.

Little oil for greasing
2 tblsp granulated sugar
4 tblsp golden syrup
1 tsp bicarbonate of soda

Lightly oil a small (7 × 10½"/18 × 25cm) Swiss roll tin or an 8–9"/20–22cm square tin. Boil the sugar and syrup in a *large* saucepan over a moderate heat, until pale golden brown. *Remove from the heat.* Add the bicarbonate of soda all at once (the mixture will froth up enormously) and stir well. Pour into the prepared tin and leave to set.

When cold and set, break into pieces with a clean hammer, store in an airtight box or tin, and eat the same day.

HOT MULLED WINE
Makes enough for 24 wine glasses; if you prefer, make 2 lots.

Very welcoming on a cold evening. It's safest drunk from paper cups. Serve it nicely warm but not too hot. Top the mulled wine up as you go along, or change to serving wine, beer or soft drinks as you prefer.

5¼ pints/3 litres inexpensive red wine
Sugar to taste – I use 2–4 tblsp
2–3 wine-glasses cheapie sherry – sweet or dry to taste
1 or 2 cinnamon sticks or 1 tsp ground cinnamon*
1 lemon – thinly sliced

Pour the wine into a large pan, add half the sugar and warm gently until the sugar dissolves. Add the sherry, taste and adjust the sugar, stir in the cinnamon sticks or sprinkle on the ground cinnamon. Taste again! Keep warm over a very, very low heat, and serve with a slice of lemon in each glass.

*If you prefer, there are lots of spice sachets now widely available which you can use instead of (or with) the cinnamon. Whichever way you make the mull, the result is wonderful.

BUT IT'S MY CAKE

8

TRADITIONAL TODDLER'S PARTY

To serve 12 children

A pleasant change from fast food burger parties!! Straightforward, familiar food that tots will find easy to eat – toddlers are often wary of trying anything new, and don't want to sit still at the table for very long once they've tasted everything that takes their fancy. Use paper plates (there are lots of super themes and patterns available to suit your child's interests), but paper cups are a bit wobbly and easily tip over, so I prefer to use pretty tumblers or cans with big straws according to the age of the participants. Cut everything really small so that the children can try lots of different things, and have plenty of paper serviettes or kitchen towel to hand for sticky fingers after tea.

Assorted Sandwiches
Chopped Lettuce * Cucumber**
Carrot Sticks * Tomato Chunks**
Sausage Hedgehogs

Cheese and Pineapple Sunshines
Savoury Clown Biscuits
Crisps 'N' Things
Butterfly Cakes *** Chocolate Krispies
Individual Candle Cakes
Jellies

Train Birthday Cake with Chocolate Finger Rails

Fizzy Drinks *** Blackcurrant Juice *** Fruit Squash

CHECK LISTS

A lot inevitably needs to be done at the last minute, but do as much cooking as possible in advance as you'll want to spend some time with your excited toddler while making final preparations on the day.

THE MONTH BEFORE
Buy and Store: Paper table cloths and serviettes (put a plastic cloth, thick old table cloth or folded cotton sheet underneath to protect your table), paper plates, straws, cocktail sticks or toothpicks, paper jelly bowls, cake cases.
   Make and Freeze: Butterfly Cakes, Chocolate Krispies and Individual Candle Cakes.

THE WEEK BEFORE
Buy and Store: Crisps, etc., or whatever is the current favourite, chocolate finger biscuits, savoury biscuits for 'clowns', jelly tots and smarties, the Train Cake (available from large supermarkets), fillings for sandwiches, salad ingredients, sausages, cheese and pineapple slices.

THE DAY BEFORE
Make the Train Cake if not pre-bought. Boil the eggs for sandwiches, shell and store in the fridge. Wash the lettuce and store in a plastic bag in the fridge. Cook the sausages, cool and store in the fridge. Make the jellies, and leave in a cold place to set. Buy cut loaves for sandwiches. Cut the cheese into dice and store in the fridge.

ON THE DAY

Hooray for Play Group!! Or persuade Granny or a good friend to mind your toddler for an hour while you prepare the food and set the table without a 'helper' taking everything off again. Defrost and finish the cakes and prepare the rest of the party menu. Set the table. Put out prizes, presents and party games ready for your little guests.

ASSORTED SANDWICHES   *Plenty for 12 children.*

Make up a mixture of brown, white and mixed sandwiches to suit all tastes, cut into various shapes, and hopefully each child will find something he or she likes. Serve a few salad ingredients separately. Don't worry if the children don't eat too many sandwiches. There are usually plenty of willing Mums and Dads to help out when they come to collect their off-spring!

1 large white thin sliced loaf
1 large wholemeal or granary thin sliced loaf
1 × 250g pack softened butter or low fat spread

Cut the crusts off the bread before you spread the butter. Make the sandwiches in each chosen filling. Cut into tiny squares, triangles, fingers and rounds (use a pastry cutter), arrange on serving plates, cover with cling film and keep in a cool place until tea-time.

FILLINGS

Egg Mayonnaise: 3 hard-boiled eggs (simmered in boiling salted water for 10 minutes), shelled and mashed with a little mayonnaise or salad cream, and/or a little tomato ketchup if that suits your child's taste!

Cooked Ham: ½ lb/225g thin sliced ham or other cooked meat.

Tuna: 1 × 7 oz/200g can tuna in oil or brine, drained and mashed with a drop of vinegar or a little mayonnaise to make a spread.

Peanut Butter: Plain or crunchy, according to preference.

Cheese: ½ lb/225g mild Cheddar cheese, grated and mixed to a spread with a little softened butter.

CHOPPED LETTUCE

Wash and dry a few crisp lettuce leaves, shred finely, pile into a bowl, cover with cling film and store in the fridge.

CUCUMBER

Wash half a cucumber, cut into thin slices, arrange in a bowl or plate, and cover with cling film until needed.

CARROT STICKS

Wash and scrape 3 or 4 large carrots, slice into thin finger sticks and pile onto a plate. Cover with cling film until needed.

TOMATO CHUNKS

Wash 4 or 5 tomatoes, slice into small segments, dish into a bowl, and cover until needed.

SAUSAGE HEDGEHOGS   *Serves 12 children.*

Use a 'hedgehog-shaped' oval potato as the base.

Preparation and cooking time: 30 minutes.

1 large oval shape potato
1 lb/454g chipolata sausages
Cocktail sticks or toothpicks (the latter are less sharp)
Lettuce or cress

The sausages can be cooked the day before. Prick the sausages and either put into a roasting tin and cook in a hot oven (200°C/400°F/gas 6–7/fan 190°C) for about 15–20 minutes, turning to brown all sides, or cook under a hot grill for 5–10 minutes until crisp and brown. Put to drain and cool on kitchen paper and store in the fridge or finish the hedgehog.

To serve: Wash the potato well, slice off the base of the oval so that the potato sits flat on a serving plate. Cut each cooked sausage into 2 or 3, spear onto a cocktail stick or toothpick and stick into the potato to make a bristly hedgehog. Arrange a little chopped lettuce or cress to look like grass on a serving dish and carefully arrange the hedgehog on the 'grass'. Keep in the fridge until ready to serve.

CHEESE AND PINEAPPLE SUNSHINES
Serves 12 children.

Bright golden platefuls! Most children like cheese, but some may not like pineapple, so I would provide more cheese than fruit. The children will enjoy eating the sun – as long as you tell them what it's supposed to be!

Preparation time: 15 minutes.

½ lb/225g mild Cheddar cheese or Edam cheese
1 small 215g can pineapple slices in syrup or juice (rings are easier to cut than chunks)
1 grapefruit
Cocktail sticks or toothpicks (the latter are less sharp)

Cut the cheese into ¾"/1.5cm dice, not too tiny or they will split when skewered. Cut the drained pineapple into bite-sized pieces. Wash the grapefruit, cut in half and put onto serving plates cut side down. Stick the cheese and pineapple onto the grapefruits with the cocktail sticks or toothpicks and stand the grapefruits on small yellow plates (margarine lids are often yellow), or blue dishes (to represent the sky), or white dishes (to represent the clouds). You can decorate the plates with cotton wool clouds if you feel artistic.

SAVOURY CLOWN BISCUITS   *Serves 12 children.*

These need to be made fairly soon before serving as the biscuits go soft if left standing too long.

Preparation time: 15 minutes.

1 150g packet round savoury biscuits
1 250g packet cream cheese or cheese spread

Clown features
Cucumber slices
Tomato slices
Little finely chopped lettuce
Few olives (for the sophisticated, omit if you wish)
Carrot sticks

Generously cover the biscuits with your chosen cheese spread. Cut the cucumber slices into triangles for clown hats; add the lettuce to make 'hair'; make the 'eyes', 'nose' and 'mouth' with the olives, tomatoes and carrots, using your creative talents! Arrange on a plate and serve fairly soon.

CRISPS 'N' THINGS

Always popular as long as you serve what is in vogue that week! Pour a few packets into bowls and arrange round the table so that each child has a bowl within reach.

BUTTERFLY CAKES

Makes 18–20.

Quick to make and freeze well.

Preparation and cooking time: 1 hour, including cooling time.

Paper cake cases
4 oz/100g soft margarine
4 oz/100g sugar
6 oz/175g self-raising flour
1 tsp baking powder
2 eggs – beaten
Few drops cake colouring if liked
Icing
2 oz/50g butter or margarine
4 oz/100g icing sugar – sieved
Cake colouring
Coloured vermicelli

Heat the oven at 190°C/375°F/gas 5–6/fan 180°C. Put paper cases in bun tins (they keep their shape better than on a flat tray). Put all the cake ingredients, except the colouring, into a bowl or mixer, and beat really well until smooth and fluffy. Divide the mixture in half and colour each half with a few drops of cake colouring if liked. Spoon into the paper cases and bake for 12–15 minutes until risen and just firm to the touch. Leave in the paper cases and cool on a wire tray.

Make the butter icing: put the butter and icing sugar into a basin and beat until smooth and creamy. Divide in half and colour with cake colourings as liked. When the cakes are cold, cut off the tops and cut these in half to make wings. Pipe or spoon a butterfly body of butter cream on top of each cake and stick the butterfly wings onto the cream. Sprinkle with a little vermicelli if liked. Serve or open freeze, then store in a plastic box.

To serve: Defrost for 2–3 hours. Arrange on a serving dish in a single layer.

CHOCOLATE KRISPIES
Makes 18 largish or 30 teeny tiny.

Make 'normal' sized cakes in pretty, coloured cake cases, or 'magic' cakes in petit four cases.

Preparation and cooking time: 15 minutes.

4 oz/100g margarine
4 oz/100g sugar
4 generous tblsp golden syrup
1 heaped tblsp cocoa
3–4 oz/75–100g approximately rice krispies
Paper cake cases or petit four cases

Melt the margarine, sugar and syrup over a gentle heat in a large pan. Stir in the cocoa and mix well. Remove from the heat and gently stir in the rice krispies, mixing well until all the krispies are coated with the chocolate mixture. Spoon into heaps in the paper cases and leave to set. Store in an airtight tin overnight, or open freeze and then store in a plastic box in the freezer.

To serve: Defrost for 1–2 hours if pre-frozen, and arrange on a serving plate.

INDIVIDUAL CANDLE CAKES
Make one for each child.

If each child has a candle to blow out it saves a lot of heartache and tantrums as otherwise all the children always blow out the birthday child's candles. The 'proper' birthday candles on the train can be blown out at the same time. *Note:* Do have plenty of adult supervision for this exercise!!

Preparation, cooking and cooling time: 1½ hours.

Ingredients for Chocolate Tray Bake – see pages 11 and 12
Icing and Decoration
4 oz/100g sieved icing sugar
1–2 tsp hot water
Few drops food colouring or 1 tblsp drinking chocolate
Sugar flowers or animals
12 candles and candle holders and small paper plates

Beat the cake ingredients together well, and bake as directed on page 11. Remove the tray from the oven, cool for a few minutes, then turn the cake onto a wire tray, remove the paper and leave until cold.

Icing and Decoration: Put the sieved icing sugar (and drinking chocolate if used) into a basin, and mix to a runny paste with hot water. Add the food colouring to the plain icing if you wish. Pour the icing over the cake and smooth with a palette knife (dip the knife into hot water and shake before use to stop the icing sticking). Leave until set, then open freeze or finish the cakes and use the same day.

To serve: Defrost for 2–3 hours. Cut into squares (you may have some spare), and place one cake per child onto a small paper plate. Decorate each cake with a cake candle in a candle holder, and your chosen sugar decorations. Put a cake in front of each child's place on the table and let them all blow out their own candles along with the birthday child – but please have plenty of adults at the table when doing this. Any extra cake not needed for candles can be saved for 'Daddy', other brothers and sisters or 'collectors' at the end of the party.

JELLIES   *2 different-flavoured jellies.*

Best made the day before to allow time to set. Make individual
jellies set in small waxed trifle cases, or make a jelly 'rabbit' and
serve it in a field of contrasting coloured jelly 'grass'. Jellies are
best kept plain for very young children, but you can set a can of
drained fruit in the jelly and use the fruit juice with the jelly
liquid if you wish.

2 × 1 pint/600ml jellies
12 waxed paper cases or 1 jelly mould

Make the jellies according to the instructions on the packet.
Allow to cool slightly, then pour the liquid jelly into the
individual cases, making equal numbers of each flavour, or
pour one jelly into the jelly mould and the other into a basin.
Leave to set in the fridge or a cool place overnight.

To serve: Put an individual jelly at each child's place, or
carefully unmould the jelly (dip the mould into a bowl of hot
water for a *few seconds* to loosen it) onto a large plate. Chop
the jelly in the basin with a knife or fork and arrange the jelly
'grass' around the rabbit (or you could have a jelly fish in a jelly
sea). Serve helpings from these into little waxed dishes.

TRAIN BIRTHDAY CAKE

Buy an engine-shaped cake or bake and construct your own engine with a Swiss Roll, blocks of Victoria Sandwich cake, chocolate biscuit wheels and lots of icing to glue it all together.

Stand the train on a thin cake board on the table, and make a railway track around the table using finger biscuits; with smarties and jelly tots as the ballast between the lines. Make sure the rails are within reach of each child as they'll all want to eat the track. Put the birthday candles on top of the engine and use a lego man as the driver.

DRINKS

Buy enough of each drink for everyone to have the same, and allow extra cans to cover spillages. Fizzy drinks are cheaper when bought in bottles, as little ones may not drink a whole can. The little cartons of drinks may be popular too, but they can be a bit wobbly on the table and it's a good idea to have some spare straws handy.

The last thing to provide is a large bottle of sherry for the adults – easier to pour out when surrounded by toddlers than large gin and tonics!! Have fun and don't forget to take lots of photos.

9
TRADITIONAL CHRISTMAS DINNER

To serve 12 people

If this is the first time you've cooked Christmas dinner, don't panic – it's all going to turn out beautifully and taste absolutely delicious, without a lot of fuss at the last minute – after all you want to be joining in the Christmas fun, not be stuck in the kitchen all morning!

Most of the meal can be prepared in advance, and convenience food can be smartened up to taste as good as home-made. Buy a fresh or frozen turkey (there are all kinds to choose from), and, as long as you buy from a reputable supplier and follow individual instructions for defrosting and cooking frozen birds, you'll achieve a perfectly cooked dinner.

Citrus Cocktail
Roast Turkey
Bacon Rolls **** Chipolata Sausages

Great Gran's Herb Stuffing
Roast Potatoes *** Potato and Parsnip Letters
Brussels Sprouts *** Peas with Mange Tout
Bread Sauce *** Cranberry Jelly/Sauce
Turkey Gravy

Christmas Pudding
Mince Pies
Brandy Butter *** Cream and Greek Yoghurt

Alcoholic and Non-Alcoholic Drinks
Coffee or Tea
After Dinner Mints

CHECK LISTS

EARLY DECEMBER
Make and Freeze: Stuffing, Potato and Parsnip Letters, Bread Sauce, Christmas Pudding, Brandy Butter and Mince Pies.

Buy and Store: Order a fresh turkey or buy a frozen one (if there will be room in your freezer), Christmas Pudding (if not already home-made), frozen vegetables such as sprouts, peas, mange tout (if room in your freezer), Cranberry Jelly, gravy powder, cornflour, stock cubes, sherry, wines, brandy, squash, soft drinks, fruit juices, 'designer' water, teas and coffees (instant and 'proper'), paper napkins, candles, table decorations, crackers, wide cooking foil for the turkey, cling film, washing up liquid and dishwasher powders, mayonnaise, sauces and pickles for turkey suppers, and extra bread for the holiday (if you've room in the freezer!).

CHRISTMAS WEEK
Collect the fresh turkey or put the frozen turkey to defrost (check the time needed for it to be defrosted by Christmas Eve *morning*).

Buy and Store: Fresh fruit for the cocktail starter (grapefruits, oranges, kiwis), fresh vegetables (potatoes, sprouts, mange tout), salad stuffs for cold turkey suppers, bacon, chipolata sausages, cream and/or Greek yoghurt. Buy or make Mince Pies if not already frozen.

Make a timetable of cooking times for Christmas Day (see page 108). Check your cooking and serving dishes to ensure that you can juggle your tins and baking dishes to fit into the oven when planned. Check your arrangements for keeping food warm while dishing up – hot trolley, plate warmer (electric or candle) or above the stove, while also allowing room for warming plates.

DECEMBER 23rd
Defrost the stuffing for inside the turkey; leave the other stuffing in the freezer.

CHRISTMAS EVE – all day, not just the evening
Assemble the Citrus Cocktail ingredients, prepare and leave in a covered bowl in the fridge.

Make the stuffing (if not pre-frozen), prepare and stuff the turkey. Put the turkey in a large roasting tin, cover with foil and leave in a secure, cold place (larder or closed garage).

Make the Bacon Rolls, prick the sausages, put onto a baking tray and store in the fridge. Peel the potatoes, leave in a saucepan of cold water. Make the Potato and Parsnip Letters if not pre-frozen. Prepare the fresh sprouts and mange tout, and store in the fridge. Check that you remembered to buy all the frozen vegetables!

Make the Bread Sauce if not pre-frozen, and leave in the fridge. Find the jar(s) of Cranberry Jelly. Cook the turkey giblets ready for gravy (or to cut up for the cats if you can't face them like me!). Mix the gravy, do not cook, but store in the fridge.

Check the Christmas Pudding (I once found mine had gone mouldy and had to dash out and 'borrow' one from a very kind neighbour), and put it ready to boil or steam. Make sure you've got enough tea, coffee and cream! Find the After Dinner mints you hid from the family. Put the holly sprig, brandy and matches ready for lighting the pud.

Put Ready – Or Find: Set the table if you don't need it for breakfast, or put ready the tablecloths, table mats, table napkins, candles, crackers and table decorations (leave floral decorations in a cool place). Set out the plates, dishes, glasses, cutlery and serving dishes.

Defrost Overnight, ready for Christmas Day: Herb Stuffing,

Potato and Parsnip Letters, Bread Sauce, Mince Pies and the Brandy Butter.

SUGGESTED CHRISTMAS DAY TIMETABLE

I'm timing dinner for 2.00 pm to allow time for Christmas Morning church and/or socialising – adjust your timetable as necessary.

You will need about 30 minutes for dishing up so time things to be cooked between 1.30 and 1.45, and try to keep everything as warm as possible. I'm assuming you only have two oven shelves to use (the turkey will take up most of the oven!), so if you have a double oven or a microwave, that's a bonus – use them to your best advantage.

8.15
Heat the oven at 180°C/350°F/gas 4–5/fan 170°C, or as instructed on the turkey wrapper.

8.30
Put the turkey on the lower shelf of the oven.

Prepare or dish the Citrus Cocktails, and leave in the fridge.

Whip and dish the cream, dish the Greek yoghurt, dish the Brandy Butter, and leave all covered in the fridge.

Dish the Cranberry Jelly, and leave covered in the fridge.

Put the white wine in the fridge, open the red wine to 'breathe'.

Check or set the table, and put the plates and dishes to warm.

10.45
Put the stuffing on the top shelf of the oven.

11.45
Take the cooked stuffing from the oven, and keep warm.

Put the Bacon Rolls and sausages on the top shelf of the oven.

12.15
Dish the Bacon Rolls and sausages, and keep warm.

Put the Roast Potatoes to parboil, heat oil in a roasting tin.

12.30
Put the Roast Potatoes on the top shelf of the oven.
Put the pudding on to boil or steam.

1.00
Heat the Bread Sauce on the floor of the oven.
Remove the foil and papers from the turkey to let it brown.

1.20
Finish and dish the Bread Sauce, and keep warm.

1.30
Dish the Roast Potatoes, and keep warm (uncovered).
Cook the Potato and Parsnip Letters on the top shelf of the oven. Turn the oven up to 200°C/400°F/gas 6–7/fan 190°C when the turkey is taken out.
Dish the turkey, leave to rest covered with foil (the turkey, not you!). Put the stuffing, Bacon Rolls and sausages in the oven with the Potato and Parsnip Letters to reheat if necessary. Remove with the potatoes, ready to serve.
Cook the sprouts, drain, dish and keep warm.
Cook the peas and mange tout, drain, dish and keep warm.
Make the gravy, and leave in a saucepan to reheat before serving.

1.45
Remove the Potato and Parsnip Letters from the oven and keep warm.
Put the starter on the table, and open the wine.

2.00
Sit down to enjoy a well earned Christmas Dinner.

2.15
Remove the starter dishes. Carve the turkey and serve the main course.
The oven should now have cooled, so put the Mince Pies to warm with the oven on its lowest setting.
Check the water in the pudding saucepan, refill if needed.

3.00
When ready, dish and light the pudding, and serve with creams and Brandy Butter.
   Serve the Mince Pies.

3.30
Relax while the others wash up and prepare the coffee!

CITRUS COCKTAIL   *Serves 12.*

A light appetizer before a heavy meal – although we go straight to the main course as we've usually been to our neighbour's wonderful 'drinks and super nibbles' party before lunch!
   Prepare the cocktails in advance and serve well chilled. If you're short of glasses, serve in the grapefruit shells.

Preparation time: 30 minutes. Chilling time: at least 1 hour.

6 grapefruit – yellow, pink or a mixture
**6 sweet oranges or 2 × 300g cans mandarine orange segments, or
   a mixture of each**
2–4 kiwi fruits
3–4 tblsp sugar to taste
12 tblsp sherry or white wine (optional)
Thinly peeled orange zest to garnish

Cut the grapefruit in halves, remove the segments and put into a mixing bowl. Wash the oranges well and pare off thin peelings of orange zest for garnish, cover these in cling film and reserve. Peel the oranges, divide into segments, or drain the canned fruit and mix with the grapefruit. Peel the kiwi fruit, slice or cut into chunks and add to the fruit mixture with the sugar. Cover and store in the fridge.

To serve: Spoon the mixture into the grapefruit shells (serrate the edges to look pretty) or glasses. Pour a spoonful of sherry or wine over each (if used) and decorate with orange zest.

ROAST TURKEY

Decide how many servings you want from the turkey – is it just a hot turkey dinner, or do you want cold meat for salads and sandwiches later? Allow approximately 12 oz/350g uncooked weight per serving, so a 12–14 lb/5.5–6.5kg turkey should give 12 generous helpings and cold meat for Boxing Day.

Calculate the defrosting time for the turkey to be ready to prepare on Christmas Eve; make sure it is thoroughly defrosted. Remove the bags of giblets, turkey neck bones, etc., which you will find inside the bird (wear rubber gloves if this worries you) and put aside for gravy. Rinse the turkey inside and out with cold water and dry with kitchen paper.

Traditionally, turkey was stuffed with sausage meat in the neck and herb stuffing in the body, but it is now not thought good to put a lot of stuffing inside poultry due to problems with cooking the meat thoroughly, so I usually put 2–3 tblsp stuffing into the body cavity and just 1 tblsp into the neck to keep the bird moist and full of flavour. Cook the rest of the stuffing separately in an ovenproof dish. If you don't want to risk any stuffing in the bird, put a small, peeled potato with 1 tblsp dried herbs in the body cavity to keep the meat moist and flavoursome.

Grease a large, deep roasting tin with vegetable oil (there will be lots of juice), and put the turkey in the tin. If it is *not* a pre-basted bird, put flakes of butter over the bird or brush with oil. Cover the turkey with buttery papers (saved from butter or margarine), take a really large piece of cooking foil, and cover the turkey and roasting tin completely, fastening the 'tent' under the rim of the tin.

Calculate the cooking time according to the instructions on the wrapper so that the turkey will be cooked and ready to come out of the oven 20–30 minutes before you want to start the meal.

Approx. cooking time: 12–14 lb/5.5–6.5kg turkey – 4–5 hours.

Oven temperature: 180°C/350°F/gas 4–5/fan 170°C.

Remove the foil and papers for the last 30 minutes of cooking time to allow the turkey to crisp and brown nicely.

To serve: Take great care: the tin will be full of hot juices. Carefully put the turkey onto a hot serving dish (use a fish slice and another pair of hands to hold the top of the turkey with a clean, dry tea-towel), cover with the warm foil and leave to relax for 15–20 minutes before carving.

GREAT GRAN'S HERB STUFFING
Serves 12 very generously.

Use any mixture of herbs for this stuffing – traditionally, sage and onion goes with pork, thyme and parsley with poultry, but I usually make a glorious mixture. Amounts are flexible; if you like lots of cold turkey, stuffing and cranberry sandwiches, make double the quantity of stuffing given here as it will keep in the fridge with the cold meat.

Preparation and cooking time: 1¼ hours.

2–3 onions
4–5 slices bread – white or brown or a mixture
8 oz/225g herb stuffing mix – flavour to taste
2–3 tblsp mixed dried herbs
Large handful fresh chopped parsley (if possible)
2 tblsp lemon juice (optional)
Salt, pepper
2 oz/50g butter

Peel and chop the onions, put into a saucepan with ½ pint/300ml hot water, bring to the boil and simmer for 10 minutes until soft. Make the breadcrumbs – use a grater or a blender. Remove the onion from the heat, stir in the stuffing mix, breadcrumbs, herbs and lemon juice, adding extra hot water as needed to make a stiff mixture, seasoning well with salt and pepper. Leave to stand for 10 minutes, then use 3–4 tblsp to stuff the turkey and put the rest of the stuffing into a well greased ovenproof dish, and dot with butter.

To freeze: Put 3–4 tblsp stuffing (to go inside the turkey) into a small container and freeze separately. Cover the dish of stuffing and freeze separately.

To cook and serve: Bake for 50–60 minutes in a hot oven (180°C/350°F/gas 4–5/fan 170°C) for 20–30 minutes. Serve hot around the turkey.

BACON ROLLS

Allow 1–2 per person.

Preparation and cooking time: 25–35 minutes.

1–2 streaky bacon rashers per person – smoked or green to taste

Cut off the rind, roll each rasher tightly and place on a baking tin, sitting on the join so that they don't unwind.

To cook and serve: Bake in a hot oven (180°C/350°F/gas 4–5/ fan 170°C) for 20–30 minutes. Serve hot around the turkey.

CHIPOLATA SAUSAGES

Allow at least 2 per person.

Preparation and cooking time: 20–30 minutes.

Prick each sausage, and put in a baking tin (with the Bacon Rolls).

To cook and serve: Bake in a hot oven (180°C/350°F/gas 4–5/ fan 170°C) for 20–30 minutes. Serve hot with the turkey.

ROAST POTATOES

Serves 12.

Preparation and cooking time: 1 hour.

6–6½ lb/3kg potatoes
Oil or dripping for roasting

Peel the potatoes, cut into even-sized chunks and cook in boiling, salted water for 5–10 minutes. Put enough fat to just cover the base of the roasting tin and heat on the top shelf of the hot oven above the turkey (or ideally at 200°C/400°F/gas 6–7/fan 190°C) for 45 minutes. Drain the potatoes, shake dry in the pan over the heat, then put into the hot roasting tin (watch for hot, fatty splashes), and roast at the top of the oven for 50–60 minutes, until crisp and golden brown.

To serve: Put into a hot serving dish and keep warm without a lid, until needed.

POTATO AND PARSNIP LETTERS   *Serves 12.*

Preparation and cooking time: 45 minutes.

3 lb/1.25kg potatoes
3 lb/1.25kg parsnips
4 oz/100g butter
1–2 egg yolks – beaten
Salt, pepper, nutmeg

Peel the potatoes and parsnips, cut into small chunks and simmer in boiling, salted water for 10–15 minutes until soft. Drain and mash until lump-free, and beat in the butter and egg yolks to make a stiff paste (don't let it get too soft to hold its shape). Season well with salt, pepper and nutmeg. Well grease a baking sheet. Put the mixture in a forcing bag with a ¾"/2cm pipe, and pipe an initial for each guest (or pipe or fork the mixture into rosettes or castles if you prefer). Cover and put aside or freeze.

To cook and serve: Defrost. Bake on the top shelf of the hot oven above the turkey (or ideally at 200°C/400°F/gas 6–7/fan 190°C) for 10–15 minutes. Turn the oven up to the ideal temperature once the turkey is cooked.

FROZEN PEAS

Allow 3 oz/75g per person; 2–2½ lb/1–1.25kg for 12 people.

Cook from frozen in boiling, salted water with a sprig of fresh mint if you have any. Drain well, stir in 1 tsp sugar and serve topped with a knob of butter and sprigs of mint if available.

MANGE TOUT

Allow 1–2 oz/25–50g per person, mixed with peas; 1 lb/450g or more if you wish for 12 people.

FRESH
Top, tail and wash the pods, cook whole in a little boiling, salted water for 2–3 minutes (they should still be crunchy when cooked), or cook with the peas. Drain and serve mixed with the peas.

FROZEN
Cook and serve with the frozen peas. Drain together, dish and keep warm until required.

CRANBERRY JELLY/SAUCE   *Allow 2 × 300g jars.*

You can make this yourself if you have an old family recipe, as cranberries are sometimes available here in November, for American Thanksgiving, but it's usual and quite acceptable to use the jars of Cranberry Jelly (smooth), or Cranberry Sauce (with bits in), which are found in most supermarkets. Tip the chosen sauce into serving bowls and serve cold.

BRUSSELS SPROUTS

FRESH
Allow 4 oz/100g per person; 3–4 lb/1.5–2kg for 12 people.

Choose small, even-sized sprouts. Trim and wash the sprouts, and put aside in a cool place until needed. Cook in a minimum of boiling, salted water for 5–10 minutes, until just crunchy. Drain well, sprinkle with a few split almonds (see page 15) and keep warm until needed.

FROZEN
Allow 3 oz/75g per person; 2–2½ lb/1–1.25kg for 12 people.

Cook from frozen in boiling, salted water for 4–5 minutes. Serve sprinkled with split almonds if liked (see page 15), and keep warm until needed.

BREAD SAUCE
Allow 2 pints/1 litre for 12 people.

Save time by using packet sauce, which gives excellent results, especially if you add a few extra ingredients! Make 2 pints/1 litre sauce as instructed on the packs, and beat in 6–8 tblsp double cream and 2 oz/50g butter. Serve at once, or freeze in a covered, ovenproof dish.

To serve: Defrost thoroughly, stir well and reheat on the bottom shelf of the oven (180°C/350°F/gas 4–5/fan 170°C) for 15–20 minutes, or ideally in the microwave until hot. Stir a little more cream into the hot sauce if you feel very indulgent, and keep warm until ready to serve.

TURKEY GRAVY   *Allow 2 pints/1 litre for 12 people.*

Use the liquid from the turkey giblets and the juices from the roasting tin after the turkey is cooked to give a wonderful flavour. We like thick gravy; if you prefer it thinner use less cornflour and gravy powder.

Preparation and cooking time: 10 minutes.

Medium thick gravy
2 tblsp cornflour or flour
2 tblsp gravy powder
2 turkey or chicken stock cubes
1–1½ pints/600–900ml water from turkey giblets
1 large glass sherry, wine or cider (optional but nice)
1 pint/600ml juices from the turkey after cooking

Mix the cornflour or flour and gravy powder with a little cold liquid (water or booze) to make a smooth paste – it must be cold liquid or the paste will go lumpy. Add the crumbled stock cubes and the rest of the liquid (apart from the turkey juices), stir well and store in the fridge.

When the turkey is dished, take the gravy mix from the fridge and stir well (the thickening will have settled). First carefully pour off the fat from the turkey juices into a basin (keep for dripping), then pour the juices into the gravy mix and stir. Pour the gravy into a pan and bring gently to the boil, stirring all the time until the gravy is smooth and thick, adding extra liquid if needed. Serve at once, or leave in the pan and reheat, stirring well, when needed. Pour into a gravy boat and serve.

BRANDY BUTTER

Serves 12.

Equally delicious made with rum and white sugar, or sherry.

Preparation time: 10 minutes.

6 oz/175g butter (unsalted if possible)
12 oz/350g soft brown sugar
1–2 sherry-glasses brandy – or to taste
Pinch grated nutmeg, cinnamon or mixed spice

Cream the butter, beat in the sugar until creamy, then beat in the brandy and spices. Pile into a serving dish and keep in the fridge, or freeze to defrost and serve on Christmas Day.

CREAM AND GREEK YOGHURT

I would allow 1 pint/600ml double cream and ½ pint/300ml Greek yoghurt, unless your family has a preference for one or the other.

Whip the cream until thick, pour into a serving dish, cover with cling film and refrigerate until needed.

Pour Greek yoghurt into a serving dish, cover and store with the cream until needed.

CHRISTMAS PUDDING

Serves 12.

Either buy a good quality 3 lb/1.5kg Christmas pud or use my easy recipe and have a go at making your own. It's simple to make; the hardest part is collecting the numerous ingredients. The cooking, however, is tedious; it takes a long time to boil or steam. I cook it in the evening when the kitchen is empty as it's a rather steamy procedure. If you have a pressure cooker, follow the manufacturer's instructions.

The pud should be made several weeks in advance, cooked and stored in a cool place – it does not need to be stored in the fridge. It then requires heating for about 2 hours on Christmas Day.

If you use silver charms or coins in your pudding, remember to warn everyone before they start eating, and take care with children to make sure they don't swallow them.

Preparation time: 30 minutes.
Cooking time: 7–8 hours.   *Reheating time: 2 hours.*

1 × 3 pint/1.5 litre pudding basin, greaseproof paper, large piece cooking foil, large elastic band
1 lb/454g mixed dried fruit – rinsed and drained
4 oz/100g glacé cherries – quartered, rinsed and drained
4 oz/100g chopped mixed nuts
1 large cooking apple – peeled, cored and finely chopped
1 large carrot – peeled and grated
4 oz/100g self-raising flour
½ tsp mixed spice
½ tsp nutmeg
½ tsp cinnamon
3 oz/75g fresh breadcrumbs – white or brown
2 oz/50g sugar – white or brown
2 oz/50g vegetarian or beef suet
2 large eggs – well beaten
1 orange and/or lemon – well washed
1 wine-glass sherry/rum/brandy, etc
1 tblsp black treacle to colour (optional)
Silver charms or coins, wrapped in foil (optional – see above)

Grease the basin well. Put the dried fruit, cherries, nuts, apple and carrot into a large mixing bowl and stir. Sieve the flour and spices onto the fruit, stir in the breadcrumbs, sugar and suet. Mix with the beaten eggs, grate the orange and lemon rind onto the pudding mixture, squeeze the juice and add enough to give a soft dropping consistency. Add the chosen booze and black treacle and mix really well – and check the recipe to make sure you haven't left anything out! Let everyone have a stir and a wish, mix in the charms or coins and pour the mix into the prepared basin.

Cover with greaseproof paper (put a pleat in the middle to open if the pudding rises) and secure with an elastic band. Wrap the basin completely in foil, and boil or steam in a pan for 8 hours (as the water boils away, fill the pan up with water from a hot kettle) or cook in a pressure cooker. When the pudding is cooked, allow to cool. When quite cold, remove the foil and paper and replace with fresh, dry covers. Store in a cool place.

To heat and serve: Boil or steam the bought or home-made pudding for about 2 hours, filling up the water in the pan as needed, or reheat in the pressure cooker. Carefully remove from the steamer, unwrap and tip onto a warm serving plate (mind the steam). Top with a sprig of holly, pour a little warm brandy over the top of the pudding and flame with a match.

MINCE PIES

Makes 24.

Home-made mince pies, with bought or home-made mince-meat, are extra delicious. If you don't have time to make your own, buy good quality ones from a reputable maker.

Preparation and cooking time: 1–1½ hours.

**12 oz/350g flour quantity shortcrust pastry or
  1 lb/454g pack frozen shortcrust pastry – defrosted
1 lb/454g jar mincemeat (see P.S. below) or
  home-made (opposite)**

Heat the oven at 200°C/400°F/gas 6–7/fan 190°C. Roll out the pastry thinly. Cut 24 rounds with a 3"/7.5cm cutter and an equal number of 2½"/5cm rounds for tops, re-rolling the pastry scraps. Put the large rounds in patty tins, and put 2 tsp mincemeat in each. Cover with the tops and press the edges down lightly. Brush with milk and sprinkle with a little castor sugar on top if liked. Prick the tops (traditionally three times) with a fork.

Bake in the hot oven for 12–15 minutes until the pastry is lightly coloured. Cool slightly in the tins, then lift onto a wire tray and cool completely. Store in an airtight tin for a few days, or freeze and defrost when needed. Serve hot or cold.

*P.S. Shop-bought mincemeat is much improved with the addition of a little sherry or brandy!

MINCEMEAT
Makes approx. 6 lb/2.5kg.

Can be made weeks or months before Christmas (or kept from one year for the next), but it is best if left for at least 2 weeks to mature before use.

Preparation time: 30 minutes.

1 lb/450g shredded beef or vegetarian suet
1 lb/450g cooking apples – peeled, cored and finely chopped
1 lb/450g stoned raisins
1 lb/450g sultanas
1 lb/450g currants
8 oz/225g mixed peel
4 oz/100g glacé cherries – quartered and rinsed
4 oz/100g chopped almonds or mixed nuts
1 lb/450g soft brown sugar (dark or light)
1 tsp mixed spice
1 lemon – well washed
1 sherry-glass brandy, sherry or rum – or more to taste
Clean, dry jars, greaseproof jam covers and lids

Put the suet and chopped apples into a large bowl. Rinse and dry the raisins, sultanas, currants and peel, and add to the apples. Add the prepared cherries, nuts, sugar and spice, and stir well. Grate in the lemon rind, squeeze and add the lemon juice, and add the booze to taste. Pack into the prepared jars, cover as for jam, and store in a cool place for at least 2 weeks before use.

10
HOUSE MOVING PARTY

To serve any number!

A cheerful way of saying goodbye to old friends and neighbours and thanking them for the good times you've all enjoyed together in the past – it also helps to relieve the trauma of Moving Day! We held this type of party after the removers had packed everything but the beds, which were to be collected first thing in the morning, but you could hold it the evening before the packers arrive.

Buy beer or lager in cans, and provide paper cups for wine and soft drinks. Order the appropriate number of fish and chips from the local chippy, to be packed and ready for collection when you arrive, and keep the salt, pepper, vinegar and sauces ready in the kitchen.

All you have to do then is arrange some music (either your own or borrowed from a neighbour), and go and collect the food when everyone is ready.

P.S. Leave a couple of large plastic sacks ready to dump all the rubbish and empties for recycling at the end of the party. Have fun!

INDEX

FREE

If you would like an up-to-date list of all **RIGHT WAY** titles currently available, please send a stamped self-addressed envelope to

ELLIOT RIGHT WAY BOOKS,
KINGSWOOD, SURREY, KT20 6TD, U.K.